Strengthening relationships through an awareness of
ourselves and an appreciation of how we treat others

HOW AM I
TREATING YOU?
LIVING WITH CIVILITY & DIGNITY

Ron Schmidt & John Lentz

CIVILITY
PRESS

Civility Press LLC
34305 Solon Road #10
Cleveland, Ohio 44139

How Am I Treating You? Living With Civility & Dignity

First Civility Press Paperback Edition: October 2009

ISBN: 978-0-9841789-0-2

An application to register this book for
cataloging has been submitted to the Library of Congress.

Printed in the United States of America

10 9 8 7 6 5 4 3 2 1

PROLOGUE

*"We all have likes and dislikes for people different from us.
But what is important is how we treat one another."*
President Barack Obama

Who is this book written for? It is written for everyone,
from every walk of life and from every country. Student,
teacher, leader, lover, bully, poet, worker, owner, server,
customer - from those in businesses to those in
communities, from citizens to officials, from referees to
fans - everyone who *can treat themselves and each other
better*. And this means ALL OF US!

The focus of this book is *how we treat one another*.
How we treat one another is with us every minute of the
day, in everything we do, in everything we try to do, in
everything we accomplish or fail to accomplish. From
Kashmir to Bhutan to Belize to Vietnam to Kenya to
Seychelles to Austria to America, we are people of the
world, alike in more ways than not. Whether in school, at
work, in sport, in government, as tourists, how we treat
one another affects everything, shapes an impression, and
builds a context.

The reasons for writing this book are twofold. The first

i

is to make us aware that *how we treat one another* affects our lives and others. Educating ourselves about *how we treat one another* can lead us to become more effective individuals and more productive citizens of the world. So we need to look at our own selves and our own behavior. Second, this book will not only encourage us to look at ourselves and our behavior but address how *we should treat one another*. Our hope is to offer practical ways to improve our civility and appreciation for the dignity of humankind.

In a popular movie of several years ago, *Groundhog Day,* Bill Murray plays an overbearing, aggressive, inconsiderate television reporter - a classic portrayal of someone who doesn't know how to treat anyone else. Day after endless day, he torments those around him. He is caught in an endless cycle of action and reaction which brings no resolution, only a return to the same day. His incivility causes him to miss every positive thing that is going on, even a chance at romance. Finally, Murray confronts his own dysfunction, and from this soul-searching comes an epiphany. His actions are causing the endless return to the monotony of this one day. This awareness allows him to consciously make an effort to "go beyond himself" and look at the others he affects. When the clock finally begins to go forward instead of "de´ja` vu all over again," his life, as well as the lives of those around him, changes remarkably. There is no change without facing truth. Truly, taking a look at our own lives and facing up to the challenges, to the graces as well as the more gritty stuff, is the path towards treating others with more compassion and dignity.

The lesson of this movie is not just a Hollywood fantasy. It really can be like this for many of us in our daily lives. It is true in business. Treating one another as mere pawns in the game creates its own negative context; we are trapped like so many mice on so many tread mills. Robert Sutton's recent book *The No Asshole Rule* vividly describes how extreme personalities adversely affect the productivity of those in the workplace as well as the businesses themselves. All of us, in our work, in our homes, and in our communities, should not only take responsibility for our own actions but also take the step to demonstrate appropriate behavior to neighbors, colleagues, team mates, and family members. It will make a difference. And what is true in our neighborhood is true in neighborhoods from Spain to Bangladesh. Civility matters and how we should treat one another is the most fundamental issue.

CONTENTS

CONTENTS

THE STORY

John Lentz

It was an autumn afternoon in Cleveland Heights, Ohio. Like many of the days on the north coast before Thanksgiving, warmth still lingered in the air and the leaves held their colors. The best time to be in Cleveland, many say: "so tranquil." The last pause before the harshness of winter descends.

However, on this day, the tranquility would soon be shattered by an event that rocked the community and rattled old fault lines of mistrust. A group of students from the public high school, perhaps pressed by an overzealous store owner, reacted to his suspicion of their gathering by causing significant damage to a neighborhood drug store.

RIOT BREAKS OUT AT CVS: "Eight Heights Students Arrested: 12 more are suspected in melee;" so shouted the headline to Ed Wittenberg's article in the Sun Press on Thursday, October 28, 2004. "The students, six girls and two boys, range in age from 14-17," said Police Capt. Michael Cannon. "That's just a small percentage of the total number who were involved," added Police Chief Martin Lentz (no relation to the author). Wittenberg reported that it took officers from 15

1

police cruisers to restore order. School Superintendent Deborah Delisle told the school board the Monday after the event that fighting is a grave concern and that responses are complex. "There is not one easy answer," she said. The President of the School Board, Ron Register, emphasized the need for the entire community to be involved in the effort to foster an atmosphere of peace and calm. "The way we are going to solve this problem is as a community," Register said. "The short-term answer is to increase security, but that does not approach the way we need to handle this for the long term."

A week later (Nov. 4) the Editor of the Sun Press wrote in response to Register's comments: "No, the responsibility" does not fall on the community but "on the teens themselves and more critically their parents. What's required is personal, individual responsibility."

A month later, Ron Schmidt called me. "John, meet me for a drink," he said. "I want to talk to you about starting something." Ron, a good friend, did not need to say much more to entice me for a meeting. So we met at a favorite local restaurant, Nighttown. As the conversation moved from small talk to depth, we talked about this "riot" at the CVS and who was to blame, or if blame was even an appropriate word. We talked about responsibility, race, youth, adults, and our community. We wondered if this event that had caused so much pain could possibly create a positive opportunity, could stir our imagination in a more hopeful direction. It is so easy to assess blame from a distance, so much more difficult to discern accountability as citizens in a community that we love. We shop at that CVS. We go to the movies and visit the

Irish pub across the street from that CVS. My children as well as Ron's are students or graduates of the school system. Our church is an anchor institution in Cleveland Heights. We acknowledged that perception often trumps reality. How could we hope for the future of the Heights if an incident like this might drive young families away to the outer suburbs in the sprawling growth to the east of the city? What if, instead of casting blame or wringing our hands at the "system" or "society" or "them," we began to talk about the need to strengthen relationships with everyone in the community, every age, every color, and every faith? What if we could mobilize the community to have a positive conversation about behavior, reclaiming the Golden Rule, engaging shop keepers, police, clergy, teachers, politicians, judges and students? Cleveland Heights has raised itself to this level of engagement many times before, and it was time to do it again. Ron wanted to keep it simple, saying, "It is too complex to talk about race relations or teen issues. I coach baseball and have seen behavior in adults that is appalling. I have heard shop attendants curse customers." I added, "And I have made not so nice hand signs to the person who cut me off at an on ramp to the freeway." Ron continued, "What if we engage the community to identify those characteristics that shape how we treat one another?"

IT IS SO EASY TO ASSESS BLAME FROM A DISTANCE, SO MUCH MORE DIFFICULT TO DISCERN ACCOUNT-ABILITY AS CITIZENS IN A COMMUNITY THAT WE LOVE.

We live in the wonderful community of Cleveland Heights, Ohio. While there may be communities across America that share much of what the "Heights" has and celebrate much of what the Heights celebrates, communities like it are few and far between.

Cleveland Heights is an inner ring suburb of Cleveland, Ohio. It has an amazingly diverse population and housing stock. In the north part of the city, you will find more modest homes and tight knit neighborhoods. In the south part of the city, you will find mansions sitting back along tree-lined boulevards. The racial mix is pretty much equally African-American and Caucasian. Orthodox Jews have their neighborhoods too. Name a racial-ethnic group, and you can find it in the Heights. Gay, lesbian and transgendered citizens find homes in the Heights. Neighbors may not see too much of each other during the winter season, but block parties are common in the summer and kids still play in front yards until dusk, which in June, July and August lasts until almost 10:00 p.m.

Cleveland Heights has an abundance of green space and parks. Cain Park boasts one of the finest outdoor stages in the region. In the summer the seats are packed for the theater and performances from nationally known entertainers. Cumberland Park houses a pool that has served the community for a century. Forest Hill Park was once part of Rockefeller's summer retreat, and old growth trees grace the meadow and walking trails. From morning to late at night from April to October softball is played. And almost every day of the year, some team - be it soccer or football - is practicing on the fields.

You will find Mexican, Indian, Thai, Japanese, Chinese, Middle Eastern, Mongolian, Greek, and Turkish restaurants through the various business and shopping districts. If you are in the mood for taco joints, steak houses, pubs, bars, coffee houses, and family gathering spots, you can find them easily.

We have Coventry Road. Along both sides of this long neighborhood street are specialty shops, book stores, eateries, and ice cream stores that have been the haven of teens for generations and are THE spot on the weekend to go and people watch. On Coventry is a toy store that has classic toys from 50 years ago; Coventry has one of the best and most intimate Rock n' Roll clubs in the nation.

Yes, there are the big-box stores and a large multiplex cinema, but Cleveland Heights boasts one of the premiere "indie" movie theaters in the region, and most citizens would rather shop at the local hardware store where "everybody knows your name" than at the mega-store.

In the summer, everyone goes to the huge outdoor pools, and in the winter you can see your friends at the state-of-the-art recreation center. People walk their dogs, and even on the coldest winter day the brave few are out jogging.

Our high school continues to produce students who attend every major prestigious college and university in the nation. We win state championships in track, basketball, and girl's lacrosse. Our music program is second to none. On Friday nights, the marching band music can be heard wafting on the air, creating a buzz, calling people's attention like the muezzin's call to prayer in Islamic countries.

Cleveland Heights is rich in leaders. Older community leaders mentor younger community leaders. We are good at naming the issues, coming together, and seeking solutions.

We are not perfect. All the stresses and strains of living in communities rich in diversity are present if sometimes subtle and under the surface. Yes, Cleveland Heights is racially mixed, but the schools are overwhelmingly African-American. Some white parents and upper middle class African-American parents send their children to private and parochial schools. But those who continue to support public education are zealous. Yes, there has been outward migration. Cleveland Heights has 50,000 residents but is losing population to communities farther east. Yes, we struggle to bring in new housing and business as the economy tightens and inner ring suburbs are pressed by outer ring suburbs, which can generate more tax revenue and boast brand new schools. Yes, we have been hit hard by the present housing crisis, and foreclosures have increased as the housing prices have stagnated. There are tensions, and the Heights struggles to maintain its identity as a bustling, dynamic, community. But people who live in the Heights care about the Heights. And this is why the so called "riot" led to a response: a call to Civility!

The root causes of the coarseness that seems so common are many. Ron and I are not behavioral scientists or psychologists. Rather, Ron is a business owner, and I am a pastor. We are educated people but not specialists. There was little we could add to the scientific conversation about root causes of bad behavior. And

then the word arose: CIVILITY. We might not be able
to discuss root causes of behavior, but we could begin
a conversation about how are we supposed to treat one
another. We could not write a sociological tome, but we
could lift up a vision of how we are to act in community.
Of course different cultures and age groups have different
ways of talking and acting and showing affection and
aggression. But of one thing we became convinced.
Everyone, young and old, of whatever race, creed, or
economic status, knew the words and phrases: "thank
you," "you are welcome," "I am sorry," "forgive me." We
had the firm conviction that people respond to what they
are faced with. If they feel insecure, they act out of that
insecurity. If they are feeling safe, they act out of that
reality, and the results are usually more peaceful, gentle,
and civil.

Civility is a word that is all about the politics of care
and the shaping of community. It has a retro-appeal,
conjuring memories of the simpler times when we knew
our neighbors and said "hello" to friend and stranger
alike. It has a practical contemporary edge that speaks to
the best of what Cleveland Heights was and still wants
to be - friendly, inclusive, hospitable, and able to build a
community across the lines that often drive people apart:
wealth, race, and religion. It has economic implications;
we wanted to create a new climate of doing business.
People want to shop at stores where they feel welcomed.
Personal attention and affirmation go a long way towards
customer satisfaction. Civility has had very real political
implications. In 2004 the ideological politically partisan
lines were being drawn sharper than ever. Ohio was

CIVILITY IS A WORD THAT IS ALL ABOUT THE POLITICS OF CARE AND THE SHAPING OF COMMUNITY.

becoming the bellwether battleground state that elected the President, and both parties were increasing the rhetoric of division. If we could hold ourselves accountable to that which is best in this community, we could attract new families and businesses, creating a sustainable northeast Ohio that was neither "red" nor "blue" but a microcosm of America at its best.

Ron and I left the restaurant and entered into the darkness and cold of that early winter's evening, but the glow of our conversation and the warmth of our friendship inspired us to think about what to do next.

The first step was to start talking to others. Cleveland Heights is not that big a town, and it doesn't take too long to become connected with school leaders, city officials, police officers, rabbis, pastors, and store owners. Ron is a member of a renowned and very old club in the theater district of Cleveland, The Hermit Club, and one day he invited two pastors (I was one of them), the superintendent of the Cleveland Heights / University Heights school system, a principal of one of the three middle schools, a program coordinator from Heights High, two lawyers, and members of the University Heights and Cleveland Heights city councils to join him there for lunch. We were male and female, black and white, religious and non-religious, but over lobster bisque and sandwiches we found that this topic of civility and how we treat one another resonated within and among us all. The city councilors recounted tales of public meetings gone bad with uncivil behavior and uncouth language. The lawyers shared how many fewer litigations there might be if everyone could cool down the adversarial nature of dispute. The school representatives grieved about how many young persons live in homes where civility is not practiced; it is no wonder children misbehave. We live what we learn. It was admitted that teachers, too, don't always provide role models of assertive and affirming leadership. Sometimes teachers and administrators can be just as uncivil as the kids. Both pastors embarrassingly admitted that the institution that should be grounded on the Golden Rule often fails to live up to the admonition to treat others as we like to be treated. Ron always was amazed that businesses, which earned their money through interaction with employees and customers, failed so horribly to shape their practices with civil intent. The bosses might be surly and the cashiers rude. It was, we all agreed, easy to describe the problem and easy to describe a solution: we needed to relearn how to behave.

So we talked and built the trust that was needed to work together effectively. We shared stories of our upbringing and our experiences. Much was discussed: racism, sexism, class struggles, and poverty. But all were topics bigger than we wanted to attack. Plus these were classic topics that had been hashed and rehashed for decades at community forums. Many in the group wanted to go beyond the traditional discussions that draw big crowds but don't really lead to any satisfying results. Rather, we wanted something tangible, something measurable that we could all unite around. We soon found that we liked each other and looked forward to these lunches. As with every other powerful movement, ours began with building honest relationships among people who cared for each other and who risked sacrificing their time and talent and treasure for a vision. We didn't want to become a non-profit, setting up a board and becoming a long term organization. Rather, there was passion about starting a movement, creating a buzz in the core institutions of our community. It was time to change the culture and reclaim the civility. Furthermore, we all agreed that it was not just about the behavior of children. Some teachers and parents could be just as bullying, passive-aggressive, and mean spirited as the most misbehaved child. Children and young adults often times were better behaved, more respectful, polite, and gentle, than the adults. So it wasn't a race thing or an age thing. We were truly all in this together. Blaming wasn't the answer. We were the leaders of the community. It was up to us to make a difference. It was up to us to reclaim the parameters of civil behavior and take the initiative to engage.

We talked with leaders in the field of civility, including Dr. Forni from the Johns Hopkins University Civility Project and author of the book *Choosing Civility: The Twenty-Five Rules of Considerate Conduct*. Through Dr. Forni, we located a civility project in the city of Duluth,

CHILDREN AND YOUNG ADULTS OFTEN TIMES WERE BETTER BEHAVED, MORE RESPECTFUL, POLITE, AND GENTLE, THAN THE ADULTS.

Minnesota. Three members of the Heights core group traveled to Duluth to learn more about its project and Duluth agreed to become our sister city. By now those of us who had gathered had become known as the core team, and together we developed a mission statement and articulated the goal of affirming civility as a core value in Cleveland Heights and University Heights.

The dynamics of any group of people working together usually determines the outcome. The core group was no different. It was comprised of folks with a lot of energy and a tremendous amount of passion. We were well connected in our community and could make things happen. We were passionate about making things better and making Cleveland Heights-University Heights the most civil, vibrant community in the nation.

In a short time, we sifted through the morass of societal challenges and got to work with an action plan. No authority figure reigned, only a spirit of respect for one another, coupled with an excitement of purpose.

SO IT WASN'T A RACE THING OR AN AGE THING. WE WERE TRULY ALL IN THIS TOGETHER. BLAMING WASN'T THE ANSWER.

Our strategy from the beginning was to form relationships within the four areas that affect most of our daily lives: school, government, religious congregations, and business. Individuals in the core group represented these anchor institutions. If we were to be effective, then we needed to engage others in our fields and spread the word.

After six or seven months of talking about and researching civility, the decision was made to engage the larger community in a dialogue about civility. To do so, we decided to conduct a free workshop for community leaders. We took a leap of faith, not knowing if anyone would come. Personal invitations went out, and the group held its collective breath to see what level of response we would receive.

On December 2, 2005, amid a stiff early-winter storm in Cleveland, the group conducted its first four-hour workshop. Invited community leaders arrived, and as the local paper had publicized the workshop, so did many other citizens who had not received a personal invitation. About ninety people attended in all, including the editor of the local newspaper, the mayor, members of city council, and many administrators and leaders within the school community.

The program for the morning included three speakers from Duluth who were instrumental in organizing the civility program there. Also included were personal statements from each of the core team members about what brought them to the topic of civility and why it was important to them. In addition, the group presented a "civility resolution" to the participants and asked them to sign the resolution both as individuals and on behalf of their organizations to make a city-wide commitment to practicing civility.

The program received excellent evaluations and press coverage, and the core team believed it to be a clear indication that the communities would like more dialogue and focus on the issue of civility.

By January of 2006, calling ourselves the Civility Core Team, we began organizing working meetings as a follow-up to the December 2nd workshop. The working meetings occurred on January 20th, February 16th, and April 5th.

During the working meetings, groups were formed to develop programs and activities around six themes raised during the December 2nd workshop. Dozens of individuals and organizations signed a civility resolution and encouraged people to talk about civility wherever and whenever they could. Officially launched as The Heights Civility Project, the grass root effort had taken hold and was spreading swiftly.

A series of speakers on topics such as "Reclaiming Civility in the Heights" and "Racing Across the Lines: Changing Race Relations Through Civility and Friendship" were held.

The Civility Project sponsored a logo/slogan contest. Posters of the logo were displayed in store windows and on posters. It was produced on t-shirts, wristbands, and static stickers which were given away free of charge.

Dr. P.M. Forni addressed a community forum of 300 people in August. A local rapper developed and performed raps about civility.

Heights Community Congress commended the Civility Project for its leadership in the community. The annual celebration of Dr. Marin Luther King's birthday included a prize for the best essay and poem on the theme of civility. The city rewrote all of its standard notices and correspondence to residents in a friendlier, more civil voice. City council meetings were conducted with a reminder of civility. The city of Cleveland Heights declared 2006-2007 as the year of civility. Every city building displayed the civility posters. An anonymous donor contributed the funding for the posters, t-shirts and wrist bands. At a time when you could sell your forearms to a company looking for advertising space, every recreational sports team in the Heights displayed the civility logo on their uniforms.

Walking through the streets of town, you could see people wearing the civility T-shirts. At the recreation center, the "Civility Practiced Here" poster was hung (and still hangs) on the front door. The blue wrist bands with civility pressed into the rubber graced the wrists of many a child. A website was developed with donor support. Our local newspaper, The Sun Press, contributed many news stories to the project. Our local library system backed the project and displayed the civility posters.

Perhaps the area of greatest success in that year of civility occurred in the schools. The Cleveland Heights-University Heights school district declared that the theme for the upcoming 2006-2007 school year would be "The Year of Civility." The school district hired Al Slawson, a retired teacher and coach, to coordinate civility projects at one of the three middle schools. Slawson created the Wiley Civility Ambassadors. In recent history, the relationship between middle school students and the local merchants had gone from bad to worse. After school a mass of pre-teen bodies would move wave-like from the school down Cedar Road, walking in front of the local merchants. Shop owners didn't like the students, and the students didn't like the shop owners. But within months,

Slawson's Ambassadors were meeting for breakfast with merchants, police and fire officials, city councilors, and the mayor. Things changed. The manager of the local Applebee's and the bank manager came to talk to the students about community involvement. A new Whole Foods grocery store opened and invited the Ambassadors to come and welcome the public. Where once there was mistrust, now young people were opening doors for the elderly and helping push carts full of groceries to the cars.

At the same school, Slawson began to work with the teachers on introducing a "Conscious Discipline" program, challenging teachers to work "inside-out," looking at their own issues and motivations before reacting to the issues of their students. All three middle schools in the district added civility programs to their curriculum. One of the local public elementary schools changed their school rules from the stressful "keep your hands and feet to yourself" to a more civil invitation to love learning and practice kindness.

The school system sponsored Dr. Forni's participation in the project and invited him to address all the administrators and principals at a morning planning session. It was an overwhelming success.

Civility posters were displayed throughout all the schools. One middle school principal, who was in the civility core committee, commented that educators from New York wanted more information on the Civility Project.

In the era of shock-jocks and the celebration of rudeness in movies and television, the students of the local high school chose civility as their homecoming theme. On Homecoming Friday night, a civility float graced the track around the football field as hundreds cheered.

Members of the core team addressed teachers, administrators, and support staff on civility in our schools during an in-service training. A grade school principal directed a musical on civility written and performed by the 4th and 5th grades students.

The author of the best seller *A Season of Life*, Jeffrey Marx, spoke to the Heights High football team about "How to be a Better Man." He challenged the young men to recognize and reject the "three lies of false masculinity" based on athletic ability, sexual conquest, and economic success. He encouraged the boys to allow themselves to love and be loved, to build and value relationships. Marx spoke of accepting responsibility, leading courageously, and enacting justice on behalf of others. He stressed the need to learn how to serve others. "What can I do for you?" was offered as the mantra of masculine development. Finally, Marx pushed for the young men to develop a cause beyond themselves.

IN THE ERA OF SHOCK-JOCKS AND THE CELEBRATION OF RUDENESS IN MOVIES AND TELEVISION, THE STUDENTS OF THE LOCAL HIGH SCHOOL CHOSE CIVILITY AS THEIR HOMECOMING THEME.

The following November, a year after the initial event in the drug store, the Heights Interfaith Council held their annual Thanksgiving service at Temple Emanu El, focusing on the blessing of community and the celebration of civility. Indeed, civility was catching on. Another significant change occurred in the city youth sports programs. Newspapers and radio shows often highlight the boorishness of parents screaming at refs, threatening opposing coaches, and berating the play of their children. But all of a sudden, Heights officials were mandating that parents had to show up at the pre-season civility session. They wanted them to understand that the program was for the KIDS! As with most great ideas that energize a movement, there comes a time when the energy of the leaders wanes, the financial support of a good cause dissipates in the face of even more pressing needs, and stresses and tensions strain the good will of the best- intentioned people. A closing of a beloved community school opened riffs between parents and administrators that are still felt in our neighborhoods. The superintendent, who had been very supportive of the Civility Project, got a new job in the State capital. The leaders of the civility group stayed in touch, but their lives got increasingly hectic. The great culture change sputtered and the idealism turned to the reality of the every day. And yet... and yet! The poster on the recreation center, "Civility: The Heart of the Community," reminds everyone who enters of a better way. Not too long ago, at a

OUR TIMES CALL FOR NEW WAYS OF BEING AND DEALING WITH OTHERS. THE COARSENESS OF YESTERDAY NO LONGER WORKS AND THE CALL TO COMMUNITY AND CIVILITY CONTINUES TO BECKON.

tense community meeting we heard, "Aren't we supposed to treat each other with more civility these days?" Mayors and civic leaders of neighboring cities still call to ask, "How did you do that civility thing?"

How can we measure success? It is hard. But it is hard to believe that we are not a better city because of that civility year. I know that I am different. My work is different. Ron has become a writer of numerous articles in business journals about the bottom line success of civility. I think our national culture has changed because of the tide of desiring a better way, a more civil way. Our new President speaks to the yearning in our national soul to heal old divisions, reach across the aisle, and bring antagonists to the table of conversation. Our times call for new ways of being and dealing with others. The coarseness of yesterday no longer works and the call to community and civility continues to beckon.

In the following pages, you will read about our deepest desire to keep civility central in schools, in faith communities, in businesses and politics. We believe that the story isn't over. It has just begun. From Cleveland Heights, Ohio, to you.

I

The Message
Principles of our humanity

The first five chapters offer principles
on how we treat ourselves and others
and how we and others should be
treated. When we know we can all be
better people, we will become aware of
what we can do to make our lives
and those around us better.

1

The Common Thread to Our Humanity

*Justice, Kindness & Humility
and Dignity, Unity & Civility*

John Lentz

Almost three thousand years ago, the prophet Micah, who lived in the northern kingdom of Israel, tried to keep it simple: "Do justice, love kindness and walk humbly with your God." (Micah 6:8). Does this still have relevance to our day? Does Micah's admonition make sense to a broader audience than a religious one? We think it does.

As we understand it, **justice** is about sharing economic wealth ("finding out what belongs to whom and giving it back to them") and allowing every person her or his claim to have value. **Kindness** is how we act upon recognizing the precious mark of humanity in every individual; we honor the other. **Humility** is holding whatever we believe with deep conviction but realizing that the truth is larger than anything we can conceive of. We are NOT the center of the universe.

In the first decade of the 21st century, it is time to reclaim Micah's admonition and lift up another set of related words: **dignity, unity and civility**. Dignity is about value. We may have our differences, but when any person is demeaned or ignored, we have compromised the essential gift of dignity which makes us human.

In the days before his tragic assassination in 1968, Dr. Martin Luther King, Jr. was in Memphis, Tennessee, supporting the sanitation workers of that city. The marchers held signs proclaiming, "I Am a Man!" The economic rights these workers demanded were grounded upon the non-negotiable recognition that they were, by the fact of their humanity, people of value. With simple but profound dignity, they marched and won.

Today, it seems at times as if we have forgotten that we are all just men and women desiring dignity. Individuals are lumped into constituencies, divided into partisan camps, stereotyped and neatly dismissed or too simply characterized. Dignity is a powerful force of reclaiming individual worth. Dignity demands that we dig beneath the thin soil of stereotype and see the rich mother lode of potential, possibility and giftedness.

We may have great diversity of opinions, but underlying this diversity is a common thread that binds us together in the network of creation. We need to find our central unity, focusing on those things we hold in common rather than emphasizing those things we disagree on. I remember two events that revealed to me the power of unity within diversity. The first memory was the great civic celebration in June, 2007, when the Cleveland Cavaliers defeated their rivals, the Detroit Pistons. Thousands of citizens from all over the Cleveland area gathered in the courtyard outside the arena. Watching the game unfold on big screens, the crowd was caught in the rapture of pride, joy and victory. I was in the crowd that night. Men, women and children of every race, creed, and color hugged and cried, laughed and jumped for joy. Even the rival fans from Detroit were treated with respect and playful trash-talk. That night, I caught a vision of a glorious potential. No one cared what anyone's political opinions were. No one knew anyone's sexual orientation. Race didn't matter that night.

The other memory of civic unity arose out of the ashes of profound sorrow and horror. In the aftermath of 9/11, citizens of New York came to help clear the rubble. Again, no one cared if these helpers were gay or straight, Jewish, Atheist, Muslim, Fundamentalist, female or male, young or old. The reality of this unity saved us as a people.

The dignity of each person and the unity that underlies our rich diversity are foundations of a civil society.

> **THE DIGNITY OF EACH PERSON AND THE UNITY THAT UNDERLIES OUR RICH DIVERSITY ARE FOUNDATIONS OF A CIVIL SOCIETY.**

Civility is a call to connect with each other, think the best of each other, hope the best for each other, and treat each other as we would like to be treated. These are themes common to every culture throughout history. These are words that set a foundation of common sense.

The word "civility" comes from the Latin root civis, meaning citizen. It is time to remember this word and shape our lives by it. The word "civil" is related to ordinary citizens like you and me. Civility is a grass roots movement. It cannot be imposed. It is essentially democratic and speaks to the best of our culture. It is time to reclaim civility, dignity, and unity.

Today, begin wherever you are. We are citizens of

> **CIVILITY IS A CALL TO CONNECT WITH EACH OTHER, THINK THE BEST OF EACH OTHER, HOPE THE BEST FOR EACH OTHER, AND TREAT EACH OTHER AS WE WOULD LIKE TO BE TREATED.**

communities that need to heal and move beyond the divisions that separate us. Choose to respond in ways that respect the dignity of the other, even if the other cannot quite yet accept his or her own dignity or yours. It makes a tremendous difference to your own being and to the future of your community. Let's keep it simple: dignity, unity, civility. Remember the words of the prophet: do justice, love kindness and walk with humility before God, or whatever higher power you recognize. Together, we can change the world. Focus on the things we have in common rather than our differences. In every interaction, demonstrate your respect for the dignity of the other person.

2

Taking a Hard Look at Who We Are

Our behaviors affect our relationships

John Lentz / Ron Schmidt

"No one is an island, entire of itself; every one is a piece of the continent, a part of the main...any one's death diminishes me, because I am involved in humankind; and therefore never send to know for whom the bell tolls; it tolls for thee." John Donne wrote these famous words in his book of devotions at the end of the 16th century. They are still true for us today. We are not isolated beings but people born into relationships. We may all need our alone time (I know I do!), but we always return to our families, our friends, our neighbors, our fellows workers or students.

Each day, we find ourselves in relationships with people we know and with people we don't know. How we treat one another in these relationships can make or break a day. The issues we face in our neighborhoods, in our cities, in our places of work and worship, in our parks and playgrounds, in government and politics are all based on relationships and how we treat one another.

Unfortunately, some of the time our behavior is shaped in reaction to what is different about the other person, be it skin color, personality, emotions, culture and many other factors. Furthermore, and likewise unfortunate, some of the time we are negatively judging other's behavior and not looking at our own.

For instance, we can spend time in trying to figure *why* a bully acts as he does, *why* Fred is always grumpy, *why* Tashan can bring out the angel in customers, *why* Sally disrespects others around her; but is the *why* what we are after? Usually, with individuals other than our own children (when they are young, and sometimes not even then!), we don't have control over why they act as they do. *Why* does Jane engage well with her students and John

UNFORTUNATELY, SOME OF THE TIME OUR BEHAVIOR IS SHAPED IN REACTION TO WHAT IS DIFFERENT ABOUT THE OTHER PERSON, BE IT SKIN COLOR, PERSONALITY, EMOTIONS, CULTURE AND MANY OTHER FACTORS.

doesn't? *Why* does Jim motivate those around him and Josh doesn't?

The real question as it relates to behavior is not, "Why does Frank act like a jerk?" The real question is, "Do we realize how our actions may affect those around us?" Frank may need months of psychoanalysis, but we are not in control of that. We can control ourselves, however, and that can make a huge difference.

None of us are perfect, and all of us can act and react out of motives that we are not proud of. However, we have a choice. Instead of reacting to the Franks of this world with negativity, we can demonstrate how to act and treat others in ways that are civil, are at least a better expression of what we truly believe, AND may even cause Frank to notice and change.

The first question should be to *ourselves*. "What should my behavior be like?" And with this in mind, let us take a look at how we treat one another by first looking at how we treat ourselves. Seeing ourselves objectively from a distance reveals much and offers insight into how we treat others.

Sometimes we act out of an unbalanced sense of self. Perhaps we are so caught up in our own stuff that we become the center of our own concerns. This we would define as selfish behavior. Or we are so completely

AND WITH THIS IN MIND, LET US TAKE A LOOK AT HOW WE TREAT ONE ANOTHER BY FIRST LOOKING AT HOW WE TREAT OURSELVES.

concerned with the other that we lose a sense of our own self. While often this selflessness is seen as a saintly virtue, it really isn't. Like selfishness, denial of self is not healthy either. Let's look at both selfishness and selflessness briefly and then define what a balanced life might look like, a life that is shaped by self-interest.

First, let's look at the behavior of a selfish person. A selfish person is one who acts as if the whole world revolves around him or herself. Typically, a selfish person is hiding deep insecurities and a profound feeling of inadequacy. While selfish people can be considerate of others in specific situations, their behavior won't last if the situation asks them to move beyond themselves in care for others.

On the other hand, a healthy personal life, as well as a healthy civil civic life, is shaped by a balance of

FURTHERMORE, AND LIKEWISE UNFORTUNATELY, SOME OF THE TIME WE ARE NEGATIVELY JUDGING OTHER'S BEHAVIOR AND NOT LOOKING AT OUR OWN.

self-respect and a respect for others. It is all but impossible to be in a healthy relationship, or to be a healthy citizen, if our personal life is a mess or imbalanced. The goal is to see ourselves as worthy and able participants in a community of other worthy and able participants. When we understand ourselves as one among others, all seeking to utilize our gifts to their greatest potential, we find a healthy balance of self-interest. Our interest is to build the civil society not only because it is good for others, but because it is good for our own selves.

Many of us face crushing demands at work. A friend of ours is the editor of a newspaper that has undergone design changes. Not only did she endure months of meetings for the redesign, but she was bombarded by irate readers who didn't like the changes. On top of that she had concerns for her elderly mother. Feeling overwhelmed, she had to get away and get her balance back. Recognizing and confronting issues such as these are paramount to a healthy balance for ourselves.

Unfortunately and far too often, when we finally begin to recognize our own worn-out condition and attempt some self care, we feel the shadow cloud of "selfishness" hover. But in

> **WHEN WE UNDERSTAND OURSELVES AS ONE AMONG OTHERS, ALL SEEKING TO UTILIZE OUR GIFTS TO THEIR GREATEST POTENTIAL, WE FIND A HEALTHY BALANCE OF SELF-INTEREST.**

this case the issue is not one of selfishness, but of self-less-ness. Being selfless sounds like a very good religious, civil thing to be, but it isn't. In the long run, we do no real service to our families, community, homes, and work places when we count our "self" as being worth less than others or of no worth at all. Considering ourselves too highly is a cause of imbalance. Considering ourselves too lowly is the flip side of the same coin. In neither case are we able to build respectful, helpful relationships with others.

When persons are either self-less or self-ish, an imbalance occurs; what goes for the individual person goes for groups. When any group declares itself the final arbiter of what is right and wrong, what is true, just or pure, it fails the test of balance; it is a selfish organization. When some are judged and excluded by the color of their skin, or the creed they profess, or their gender, age, nationality or orientation, the call of our humanity is not heeded. When members of the in group keep to themselves, then corporate selfishness is exhibited and the final service to the larger society is a failure. Conversely, being part of a group that defines itself by caring for the members and reaching out in concern to others can be dazzlingly liberating and powerful. We are more powerful together than alone.

OUR INTEREST IS TO BUILD THE CIVIL SOCIETY NOT ONLY BECAUSE IT IS GOOD FOR OTHERS, BUT BECAUSE IT IS GOOD FOR OUR OWN SELVES.

The great American writer James Baldwin knew well the indignities suffered by African-Americans within the larger white culture, yet he wrote, "Hatred, which could destroy so much, never failed to destroy the man who hated, and this is an immutable law." Thinking of the dignity of man, we would add, using Baldwin's words, "Civility, which can build so much, never fails to redeem

the one who is civil, and this also is an immutable law."
Like the Golden Rule, like the balance of self-respect and
respect for others, civility transforms both the person and
the culture.

3

Civility
The Bridge - How we should act

John Lentz / Ron Schmidt

Human beings have a fundamental need to be civil to one another. Whether it stems from respect or love, our civility to others goes a long way in forming relationships. Civility demonstrates how we should treat one another.

Civility is not just a legal contract between individuals but an awareness and appreciation of the complexity and diversity of our life in community and a commitment to the fact that we are one among others. I need you and you need me. Civility is the glue of our life together, the bonding agent of community.

Civility is something we need to think about daily. It is like turning on the light bulb each day, keeping the energy flowing through us into all our interpersonal networks. It must become a daily regimen like exercise and diet, best executed at a personal level but easier and less costly than gyms or special foods. We need to check the civility connections daily. Really, civility is a natural turn on!

Certainly all the major religious traditions as well as secular society in general agree on a central code of ethical conduct of how we treat one another. This generally agreed on code is usually called The Golden Rule, which states that persons should treat others as they themselves would like to be treated.

CIVILITY IS THE GLUE OF OUR LIFE TOGETHER, THE BONDING AGENT OF COMMUNITY.

JOHN:

In my tradition, Christianity, there is a corollary notion that we should "love our neighbor as ourselves." This injunction suggests that there is a close connection between care for others and self-care, and that we should see ourselves as persons to be honored just as we honor our neighbor. There is a necessary connection between treating others well and treating our self well, respecting others and respecting self, being civil to another and being civil to our own self. It makes common sense, really. How often do I realize that my uncivil act to someone else (cursing at a driver to my right when he beat me to the light!) is really caused by my own stress and my own lack of self care? Yet while I believe we generally agree on this Golden Rule idea, in my years of experience as a pastor I have come to see that many feel comfortable being nice to others even as they harbor a large dose of self-doubt. Too many people are too hard on themselves. Some think it is selfish to consider their own needs. Hence, many become burned out, used up, tired, frustrated, and even angry. Many folk think that they should never show frustration, never take into account their own "stuff." Sooner or later this unrest inside will show itself by stress-related medical conditions, or the unrest inside will show itself on the outside. You can't keep a lid on a boiling pot!

But what happens if I <u>am</u> civil, yet my civility doesn't change the situation? Sometimes we seek to be civil, and our effort is returned with incivility. That occurs frequently. However, I know that when I am living a balanced life, seeking to take my own needs seriously and still remembering that I am one among many - not more special or less - I find that I can move quickly beyond the moment, put it behind me and move on. I don't require or even expect a civil response, but I can keep faithful to my deepest sense of self and react in ways that keep me centered instead of making me feel embarrassed when I give in to my lowest common reaction.

RON:

The editor of the newspaper mentioned in Chapter 2 spent some time with a group of people in New Mexico and talked about the "angst, anxiety, worry, frenzy, and hopelessness" in her life. After returning, she vowed to "quit measuring 'success' of weekends by how much I get done, and allow myself to read, write, and be renewed without feeling guilty." This is a great place to start.

When I was a kid growing up in a southern Appalachian town, I received the gift of civility and humanity from an unexpected person, and that gift has shaped my life to this day. While recovering from surgery, I received a daily visit from a man who, in this small-town hospital, delivered newspapers to me and to the other patients. Ernie was the son of immigrants from Iran and worked in a men's clothing store. Every morning he bought enough copies of the newspaper for every patient in the mountain hospital. Ernie did it because he wanted to show each patient how important he or she was. Ernie's act of kindness and civility affected me and many others, I am sure.

This story has all the essential elements of the kind of behavior that we must all embody. Ernie was a stranger. The patients didn't know him. Yet he gave to all and all received. There were young and old, men and women, teachers and politicians, bootleggers and policemen, humble mountain folk and city sophisticates; all were greeted and given to. He valued no one more or less than the other. Amazing! The man whose parents emigrated from Iran became the *teacher* of how we should treat one another in small town America.

So in the bigger scheme of things, what role does civility play and why? Civility becomes our foundation when interacting with others, it becomes our platform that we are grounded on; it's our rock. If we try to attain unity and dignity with a weak foundation, over time the relationships will erode, our rock turns to sand. Civility grounds us in our own humanity and unites us with everyone else.

Thinking about it another way, civility is the switch that literally keeps the lights on in our communities. And yet, while few if any will argue against treating one other with respect and dignity, we have trouble keeping the lights on. Why doesn't the switch just stay on? Why do collective bodies of people - companies, organizations and communities - not even care if this value is communicated?

CIVILITY IS THE SWITCH THAT LITERALLY KEEPS THE LIGHTS ON IN OUR COMMUNITIES.

What if communities and schools espoused this value? Would more people want to live in that community and attend that school? Yes, because civility helps create relationships and nurture engagement. When we are in relationship with others, caring for them and being cared for by them, we are not as concerned with self-preservation. We are less likely to act defensively or selfishly.

There are subtle divisions in our communities and

organizations that over time become barriers to unity and dignity. For us to succeed, we must build bridges where there are barricades. Ernie was a bridge builder in that mountain hospital and community.

THE CHANGES WE WANT TO SEE IN OUR BUSINESSES, OUR COMMUNITIES, OUR SCHOOLS, OUR POLITICAL ARENAS ALL BEGIN WITH A COMMITMENT TO TREAT OURSELVES WITH GREATER KINDNESS.

Let's think about this on a bigger scale. What kind of "Ernie" like things could you do in your community, where you work, at the business you own, where you shop or go to school?

The changes we want to see in our businesses, our communities, our schools, our political arenas all begin with a commitment to treat ourselves with greater kindness. That allows us to look at our civility in all of our interpersonal relationships. And from that, we then can look at the barriers to civility and, in a spirit of ethical leadership, work to convert those barriers to bridges. That's where the magic lies; that's where the change begins, that's what we need to reconcile and act upon - now. As you read on, you will be struck by the importance civility plays in connecting and forming relationships with others.

4

Connecting with the Dignity of Humankind
Where humanity begins

John Lentz / Ron Schmidt

How we treat one another begins with how we connect with one another and how we affirm one another. Affirmation can be seen in how we make eye contact, in our body language; all of this is integral to "turning the switch on" and to keeping us connected and engaged, to <u>forming</u> a relationship. Affirmation in a work setting breaks down isolation between co-workers, and it aids social supports in a community or an organization. It's difficult to build relationships in a community, in an office, with customers without affirmation or without acknowledging others.

During our daily encounters with others we make conscious or unconscious decisions on how we interact. Some of us are introverts, some extroverts, some are passive, some aggressive. Regardless of who we are, our interaction, whether in a smile or frown, in a "hello" or looking away, tells others something about us. This same response says something about how we treat others and how we treat ourselves and is the heart of humanity to ourselves and others.

The first step in forming relations is engaging with the other person. Relations are formed when we can look one another in the eye with an out-stretched hand for greeting. In other words, how we treat others forms the backbone for our relationships.

So engaging with others is about connecting and affirming. It conveys a sense of dignity to both people. The word engagement is often defined as emotional involvement and commitment. It has emerged as a powerful quality for businesses and organizations because it speaks to an environment where people make

THE FIRST STEP IN FORMING RELATIONS IS ENGAGING WITH THE OTHER PERSON. RELATIONS ARE FORMED WHEN WE CAN LOOK ONE ANOTHER IN THE EYE WITH AN OUT STRETCHED HAND FOR GREETING.

decisions wisely. Their contributions are not driven by mandate. They are offered spontaneously because individuals believe in the value of the effort to which they are adding their energy and because barriers to engagement have been removed.

In addition to affirmation, how we talk with others is important. The bromide is true: what's important is not what we say, but how we say it. In the popular book from the 1970s entitled *Parent Effectiveness Training*, Dr. Thomas Gordon discussed the importance of "I" messages. For instance, imagine you are talking with a co-worker and say, "Fred, you don't know what you are doing. Our inventory is backing up and our customers are not receiving our products in time to serve their customers. If you don't remedy this right away, your job will be in jeopardy." Now imagine saying, "Fred, I need your help. It appears to me that our inventory is climbing and our customers can't receive timely delivery. Are there problems that I'm not aware of? How can we work together to solve these issues?" If you were Fred, which message would

THE BROMIDE IS TRUE: WHAT'S IMPORTANT IS NOT WHAT WE SAY, BUT HOW WE SAY IT.

you respond to positively, to which message would

you throw up a roadblock or barrier? If the answer is so obvious, why do we have managers out there who use "you" messages instead of "I" messages? In our communities, are "you" messages at the heart of disagreements?

This "I message" method of communication can be powerful with all people, including young people. A couple of years ago, I was teaching Junior Achievement at one of the local grade schools. On

AND AS I CONTEMPLATED THIS, I REMINDED MYSELF OF HOW KIDS, LEFT TO THEMSELVES, OFTEN ARE BETTER PROBLEM SOLVERS THAN PARENTS.

the first day, I introduced civility to the second grade class. It went over well; they really caught on and they practiced the "I" messages. That year, there was an issue before the community regarding the closing of one of the elementary schools. It was contentious and each neighborhood was protective of its school. I thought this might be a perfect opportunity for the kids to discuss civility in light of this issue. So I divided the class up, those opposing a school closing and those for it. I had each child talk about the issues as if their own school might close and had them use the "I" messages in their discussion. The discussion became so constructive that I notified the school superintendent that maybe the second graders would be good role models for the parents. And as I contemplated this, I reminded myself of how kids, left to themselves, often are better problem solvers than parents.

AS WE LOOK AT HOW WE CONNECT WITH OTHERS, MAYBE THE QUESTION IS, "HOW DO WE WANT TO BE CONNECTED WITH OTHERS?" WHAT MAKES US FEEL GOOD? I ALMOST ALWAYS FIND THAT FOLKS LIKE TO BE AFFIRMED.

As we look at how we connect with others, maybe the question is, "how do we want to be connected with others?" What

makes us feel good? I almost always find that folks like to be affirmed. In my community, I say hello to strangers all the time, at least when they look my way. During a recent visit to New Zealand, I found both men and women initiated hellos. I personally like to connect with those around me. And in my community most folks seem to respond the same way. There are others parts of our country and other countries where the response differs, and we must respect that, but in general people like to be recognized.

People who own a business or work in a business or organization risk failure if they don't affirm their customer, employees, and suppliers. That's how the world works. Without that daily connection, those relationships will falter. That is a fact. What people who choose not to affirm others are really communicating is, "you are not worth it." It may be unintentional, but the message is clear. You and I must always think of how our actions reflect on the humanity of others.

Sometimes in business - perhaps more often than we want to admit - we become so focused on the product and the price that we lose track of what got us there;

SOMETIMES IN BUSINESS- PERHAPS MORE OFTEN THAN WE WANT TO ADMIT-WE BECOME SO FOCUSED ON THE PRODUCT AND THE PRICE THAT WE LOSE TRACK OF WHAT GOT US THERE; THAT IS THE RELATIONSHIP, I.E. OUR RELATIONS WITH OUR EMPLOYEES, CUSTOMERS AND SUPPLIERS. that is the relationship, i.e. our relations with our employees, customers and suppliers. That's the connector element, that's the people part, connecting with our humanity. Sometimes we get the feeling that Wall Street dictates to us. Wall Street rewards the short term profit, Wall Street dismisses the human capital element - yes, that same Wall Street that had to be bailed out by the government. How ironic that fabled Wall Street doesn't get it. But as those of us who own businesses can attest, our people got us here. This is something we never want to forget.

So let's begin our quest for connecting by taking the first step. It comes down to having more bridges than barriers. Listening is a bridge. "Greeting people as equals irrespective of title, position, race, or creed is a bridge," notes P.M. Forni. Being inclusive of others is a bridge. Accepting responsibility and offering apologies where appropriate is a bridge.

So how do we build bridges in our communities, congregations, businesses and government, and what are the hurdles? It first begins with engagement and the "tenets of engagement" as adapted from

P.M. Forni's, Choosing Civility:
Twenty-five Rules of Considerate Conduct.
 We should:
- Listen
- Apologize
- Be aware
- Be inclusive
- Speak kindly
- Show respect
- Tell the truth
- Seek agreement
- Take responsibility
- Accept constructive criticism

These are the steps we all must take to better connect, better affirm, and better communicate with those with whom we work, live and play.

5

The Unity
of Relationships

The core of our humanity

Ron Schmidt

In the forward to Virginia Satir's book from the 1980s, *The New Peoplemaking,* the renowned family therapist stated:

"In this age of expanding knowledge about this small world of elementary particles and this very large world of extragalactic astronomy, we are also learning new things about people's relationships with people. I believe that historians a thousand years from now will point to our time as the beginning of a new era in the development of humankind, the time when people began to live more comfortably with their humanity."

Virginia Satir understood this connection over 30 years ago. And if she were with us today, I think she might add the thought, "when people gain a new appreciation of their humanity through their relationship with others, it will be demonstrated by how they treat one another."

Let's step back and think about the significance of relationships and the influence of others. In daily life, there aren't many things that we do by ourselves. We work with others, eat with others, enjoy recreation with others, and accomplish tasks with others. Of course, there are projects that only we can do and time that must be spent alone, but by and large, in what we do, day in and day out, we are dependent upon those around us in many ways.

So what do others do for us? They grow food for us, keep our homes warm for us, make cars for us, give employment to us, and teach our children for us. Relationships offer sharing of ideas, meals, books and freedoms. We build things together, make towns together,

"WHEN PEOPLE GAIN A NEW APPRECIATION OF THEIR HUMANITY THROUGH THEIR RELATIONSHIP WITH OTHERS, IT WILL BE DEMONSTRATED BY HOW THEY TREAT ONE ANOTHER."

and go to concerts together. We form teams together, build congregations together, and play music together. So being together is an end in itself.

What is the essential *foundation* of relationships? Most importantly, the tenets of engagement shared in Chapter 4 apply. There must be a willingness to engage. I know for me engaging comes naturally; for others, due to a variety of reasons, engaging is not effortless. But stop and think of the benefits. Such small things as saying hello to a stranger, making eye contact, and smiling may make someone's day, as well as your own. I was recently talking with a waitress in Europe who says she loves visiting New York because everyone says hello and goodbye in so many different ways and to everybody. She felt good to be in an environment like that. A friend of mine says "thank you" twice when he ends a telephone conversation, no matter the significance of the call. There are many small ways we can show our humanity for others. We all need to give it a try and see how it feels.

What makes relationships work? For one answer let's look at how healthy relationships affect business. As reported in the New York Times, a well-known company attributes much of its success to hiring smart people, but, more importantly, to having a flat hierarchy that encourages folks to challenge one another and to hold one another accountable for their ideas, opinions, and actions. As a result, good ideas get to the top; they are listened to and acted upon.

By contrast, as reported in the Wall Street Journal, a European concern which lost billions in a financial trading fiasco may have set itself up to fail by organizing its employees into "haves and have-nots." This bank, which traced its roots to Napoleon III in the 19th century, staked its modern future on the "quants," traders from elite French universities with advanced degrees. The actual trades, however, were executed by back-office employees with little or no contact with the top echelon. The quants' path was made quite clear to them on entering the bank's employment; they would never serve in lesser positions in the back office. The back-office trading unit was considered the lowest rung of the ladder. This "isolation" may have triggered the negative motivation of one employee "to show them (the haves) that they (the have-nots) have worth and are just as valuable as the highest executive."

A healthy relationship is one of balance and acceptance. It allows us to meet as equals, grants us each safe passage between our separate points of view, and allows us entry into each other's worlds and safe passage back to our own. In addition, it celebrates our differences and builds on our strengths. Many organizations identify the leadership qualities of each person, understanding that a balance of different styles is an asset to their development and accomplishment of goals. A baseball team of all right-handers or all power hitters wouldn't be very successful. Every group and relationship benefits from differences;

A HEALTHY RELATIONSHIP IS ONE OF BALANCE AND ACCEPTANCE. IT ALLOWS US TO MEET AS EQUALS, GRANTS US EACH SAFE PASSAGE BETWEEN OUR SEPARATE POINTS OF VIEW, AND ALLOWS US ENTRY INTO EACH OTHER'S WORLDS AND SAFE PASSAGE BACK TO OUR OWN.

they not only keep things interesting, but we tend to feed off these differences.

So how do we build an ideal team? A baseball team and the diversity that it requires is a model. The team needs different abilities: speed, power, finesse, stamina, motivation, strategy, emotional control, agility, grit and determination. It is unlikely that every single player will possess all these attributes. The goal is to build a team of people that will blend their abilities and traits into a team working for team goals. Easier said than done? Not really, but for some reason it doesn't happen very often.

Relationships are an integral part of our success in business, schools, government, congregations, and sport. As we proceed to the second half of the book, keep in mind how the success of relationships affects the success of the sectors you are in. Think about customer service in light of relationships in these groups. We'll define the

RELATIONSHIPS ARE AN INTEGRAL PART OF OUR SUCCESS IN BUSINESS, SCHOOLS, GOVERNMENT, CONGREGATIONS, AND SPORT.

"customer" loosely as the consumer of your business services, the student in your school, the resident of your community, the member of your congregation, or the kid on your baseball team. We will see how relationships are significant to all of these bodies.

II

The Message

*How we treat one
another in our daily lives*

The next five chapters apply the
principles addressed in Part I to our
lives in community, school, religion,
sport, and business. It offers the
opportunity to continue to ask the
question, "How am I treating you?"
as we go forth in our daily lives.

6

Community

How are we treating others?

John Lentz / Ron Schmidt

JOHN:

Community is a powerful word. I like to break it down into two constituent words: Common and unity. When we are in community, we have a unity in what we share in common. During the summer months, my neighborhood has a block party. It is a day of celebration and fellowship. I am always filled with a buzz of amazement. There are many different types on my block, many different opinions, political perspectives, religious or non-religious affiliations. If the neighbors who live on our particular street were scattered about the larger city, many wouldn't choose to find each other or to call each other "neighbor" or "friend." And yet we have the unity of our local space, our street. We care for the children that play in the front yard. We watch each other's houses during vacations. We borrow each other's drill bits, lawnmowers, cups of sugar and eggs. We babysit for each other's children. We have much in common even though we are, in many ways, so different. Even if we disagree on politics, we are friendly and caring to each other. There is a bond.

We find ourselves in many different types of communities, those collections of relationships that bind us together. The bonds to our congregations, to our businesses, to our schools and government and our sport teams give us identity. Truly, "no person is an island." Community is at the heart of who we are and how we want the world to be.

The love of our community brought us and several others together to discuss our collective responsibility in reclaiming civility as the foundation of our community. How we live together is shaped by how we treat one

COMMUNITY IS AT THE HEART OF WHO WE ARE AND HOW WE WANT THE WORLD TO BE. another. Our neighborhoods shape how we live together.

Our goal is to rebuild neighborhood bridges. Without bridges, barriers arise, and when barriers arise, issues of behavior and lack of civility follow in the shadows.

Consider the story of Marseille, France. Marseille is the second largest city in France, located in the south on the Mediterranean. Marseille has a significant immigrant population from Northern Africa and Eastern Europe. While unemployment plagues the city, the disparities in income and class are not segregated on the outskirts of the city, as they are in Paris. The New York Times reports that, while there is racism in Marseille, "...it's a city in which you have the freedom to move around the city if you choose." In addition, "...it is more socially conscious (than Paris)...That's because there is a real sense of community." Two years ago, while the slums of Paris erupted in violence, Marseille remained calm, perhaps because "...unlike Paris, where immigrant poor occupy huge concrete blocks cut off from the city center, Marseille has its neighborhoods, like Noailles, that are smack in the middle of town, while the hard-pressed quarters to the north are linked to the center by cheap public transport and remain inside the city limits. So residents feel that they belong to Marseille, because they

HOW WE LIVE TOGETHER IS SHAPED BY HOW WE TREAT ONE ANOTHER. do, and in turn they feel that Marseille belongs to them."

WITHOUT BRIDGES, BARRIERS ARISE, AND WHEN BARRIERS ARISE, ISSUES OF BEHAVIOR AND LACK OF CIVILITY FOLLOW IN THE SHADOWS.

A sense of belonging seems to be at the heart of this, being part of the team, feeling like a contributor, being part of the solution.

Communities are recognizing this appeal and moving in that direction. Recently the Hello, Neighbor program was initiated in Portland, Oregon, to get its residents to affirm and engage with one another. This "neighbor to neighbor" program is designed to get residents talking with one another. The High Point Initiative has been adopted in several cities in an effort to uplift communities infested with drugs by letting drug dealers and police know what unacceptable behavior is. And right in our neighboring community of Shaker Heights, the Winslow Road Initiative has given the "residents a sense of closeness, community, and common purpose since the residents began to reconnect" reported The Plain Dealer of Cleveland. All of this takes engagement.

Nestled on a hillside on the plains between Tel Aviv and Jerusalem, the community of Neve Shalom/Wahat al-Salam stands as an alternative to regional violence and strife. The "Oasis of Peace," as it is know in Hebrew and Arabic, is made up of dedicated Jews and Palestinians, all Israeli citizens, who have established a model that they hope others will see as evidence that a new kind of society is possible - one where the state of Israel is sustained, where the Arab minority owns an equal and legitimate voice, where traditions and cultures are valued together

NESTLED ON A HILLSIDE ON THE PLAINS BETWEEN TEL AVIV AND JERUSALEM, THE COMMUNITY OF NEVE SHALOM/WAHAT AL-SALAM STANDS AS AN ALTERNATIVE TO REGIONAL VIOLENCE AND STRIFE. as an integral facet of the rich history of the Middle East.

It's important that all communities look at how they treat others. Our communities of Cleveland Heights and University Heights took a look at this a couple years ago, and we are better because of it. We brought government, school, religious and business leaders together to ask the question, "How are we treating others?" We knew addressing this question would make us a better community and would make our congregations, businesses, government, and schools better. And it has.

RON:

We are more aware of how our behavior affects others in our community, how good it feels to say hello, how eye contact with others makes us feel a part of where we live. I feel comfortable making others aware when their behavior is out of bounds. I have had kids as well as adults shake my hand for reminding them. I've even been bought a couple of beers for doing it. And I've had spontaneous hugs from folks I didn't know while exchanging a story at the deli counter.

We all want to live our lives with a community sense of responsibility and respect for the dignity of mankind. Take the leap, give a smile to someone you don't know.

7

School

How are we connecting?

Ron Schmidt

Schools are places where all sorts of connections are going on all the time - student connecting to student, student connecting to teacher, administration connecting to both groups, teacher connecting to teacher and, of course, parents connecting to all the above-mentioned constituents. But how deep are these connections? The more trust and respect in the school, the higher its success and the better the learning. Success is based on the formation of community, on the articulation of a common goal, on treating others with civility. School, like business, is grounded in and on relationships. At the beginning and end of each school day, every person - student, teacher, administrator, office staff, principal, bus driver, cafeteria worker, and school board member - should ask the question, "How am I treating others?"

The relationship between teacher and student is primary. The teacher's job is to nurture and guide the pupils to give their best and discover the love of learning. The relationship between teacher and student has, in recent years, received increasing attention, and not always in a positive light. But there is no challenge to the time-honored notion that success in school is directly related to the relationship between the teacher and the student.

AT THE BEGINNING AND END OF EACH SCHOOL DAY, EVERY PERSON - STUDENT, TEACHER, ADMINISTRATOR, OFFICE STAFF, PRINCIPAL, BUS DRIVER, CAFETERIA WORKER, AND SCHOOL BOARD MEMBER - SHOULD ASK THE QUESTION, "HOW AM I TREATING OTHERS?"

What model is most effective

in educating students? I have asked high school students this many times. Those teachers who connect the best, engage the best, and care the most are seen as the best model for education. Engagement and connection are key, whether in business, religion, sport, school or community. When we don't have an effective relationship, we don't have an effective educational model. What can we do to ensure the success of this model?

The issue of "bad" behavior in the classroom seems to be getting lots of attention these days. Let's start with the student's behavior and the school's responsibility. The schools must communicate standards for acceptable behavior and unacceptable behavior. Regardless of the student's home life or external environment, setting standards of behavior for all students comes first and foremost. The school needs to take this leadership role. And yet the articulation of a set of standards does not have to be heavy handed. In one school, the code of conduct used to be "keep your hands to yourself." It's not a bad thing to remind students of this and to hold them accountable, but this statement sent a negative message. In this same school, the principal re-wrote the code of conduct: "Respect yourself and others," "Enjoy learning," and "Treat others with civility." In this school, these positive messages have gone a long way in creating an atmosphere of community.

Next, let's take a look at the role of the teacher. The teacher sets the tempo in the classroom. The relationship between teacher and student breaks down when there is poor communication and a lack of respect. Both student and teacher must abide by the rules of engagement. A

BOTH STUDENT AND TEACHER MUST ABIDE BY THE RULES OF ENGAGEMENT. A DISRESPECTFUL TEACHER DOES INORDINATE DAMAGE. TEACHERS NEED TO SET THE EXAMPLE. STUDENTS WILL FOLLOW.

change can be hard. However, as our local school system participated with the Civility Project, administrators, teachers, and staff found ways to break bad old patterns and establish good new ones. At one middle school, for instance, the principal realized that the teacher who had the most difficult relationships with students continually misinterpreted their hip-hop language and behavior. As a result, he was offended and judgmental when students actually didn't intend any disrespect.

"A student would say 'what up, my dog?' and attempt a hip-hop handshake with the teacher, and right away he'd send the kid to the office," explains former principal and Civility Project leader Renee Cavor. "I had to explain that while this form of address is not appropriate, it's actually a form of endearment. Instead of getting angry, the teacher started to pull the kids aside - so he didn't embarrass them in front of their friends - and explain that such language isn't appropriate with adults. That teacher turned around and became one of the coolest teachers, according to the kids. It was because he started to understand the world of adolescents. When he understood them, he could mold them and guide them."

All the teachers and staff at this middle school were challenged to examine and improve the ways they modeled civility to the students, and to acknowledge it when they didn't. For instance, at one very emotional ball game a coach got into a nasty argument with a parent. Students watched the fight with excitement, directing all their energy to the kind of behavior that the Civility Project was trying to change and talking about the fight long after the game ended. Realizing his mistake, the coach made a public apology to the school the next day and said he would never want his athletes to behave like that. "It meant a lot to the students to hear the coach own his mistakes and take responsibility," says Renee Cavor. "That was a great lesson for everyone."

Monticello Middle School also incorporated twenty-minute lessons about civility into student lunch periods, in which home room teachers led discussions on nine major topics based on a curriculum created by the Duluth, Minnesota, Civility Project: paying attention, listening, being inclusive, breaking the chain of gossip, showing respect, being agreeable, apologizing, giving constructive criticism, and taking responsibility. As these lessons proceeded,

ALL THE TEACHERS AND STAFF AT THIS MIDDLE SCHOOL WERE CHALLENGED TO EXAMINE AND IMPROVE THE WAYS THEY MODELED CIVILITY TO THE STUDENTS, AND TO ACKNOWLEDGE IT WHEN THEY DIDN'T.

along with improved teacher and staff modeling and other measures, the culture inside the school began to transform. In 2009, the school received the prestigious Ohio Department of Education's "Ohio Schools to Watch" designation.

We cannot leave out the influence of the parents on civility in our schools. As many in education have witnessed, the school's policy on behavior may be at odds with how students are treated by their parents at home. The school / teacher's influence on the students' behavior stops when they go out the school door. So what to do? While some teachers may make home visits in an effort to establish relationships with the parents, it is not the role of the teacher to instruct parents on how to interact with their children. But when parents are on school grounds, appropriate behavior should be expected from them. As a direct result of our local school system's participation in the community's civility project, one middle school principal reported that her students would "suggest" to their parents when their behavior became unacceptable during a parent / student meeting with the teacher and administrator. In this case, the student became the teacher for the parent.

It is amazing what positive messages can do. At one middle school, students became community ambassadors. They were encouraged to take a moment to introduce themselves to the merchants whose shops they walked past on their way home from school. Merchants were tipped off that this would happen so that they could be ready to welcome the visits. Children who were once eyed with suspicion were now viewed as good kids. The merchant could actually go out and say "quiet down" to these same kids later and have his request respected. These same young people were invited to city council meetings to get to know the local politicians. These are very simple but profoundly powerful examples of what can be done to change the culture and to build community based on civility.

To some extent we can apply a business model to schools. As public schools compete with private and charter schools, viewing the student and parent as customers makes sense. While this is a paradigm shift that many schools are involved in, the answers are difficult, every school is different, and schools aren't businesses. Nevertheless, there are parallels. Change always starts with a vision from the leaders and then moves both top down and bottom up. In school, that vision must comprise both high academic standards and the bedrock human values of respect, kindness and generosity.

How we roll out that vision depends on facts and circumstances. It depends on the superintendent and principal who prioritize and appreciate the mix. As Don Keough, the past president of Coca-Cola explained, when asked to give a talk on business success, "Every business is different. A formula for one company's success won't translate to another." So instead his speeches parallel his recent book *The Ten Commandment for Business Failures*, where he outlines surefire ways to fail.

Talk of failure is often seen as counterproductive, but rephrasing this in a proactive approach may be beneficial. We'll try a different spin to avoid failures.

For all those who are with our students, let's try to abide by the following:

• Be team players: everyone likes to be part of the whole.
• Connect with students: show that you care about them everyday.
• Communicate often: parents and students need to hear from you.
• Decide on the best way to teach math: but remember it may be easier to find a cure for cancer.
• Ask for help: we are happier when we reach out and collaborate.
• Love the kids: you were once one.
• Reward all kids: you never know who will end up on American Idol.
• Motivate and lead: everyone benefits from it.
• Believe that it's okay to not always know the answer: be honest to yourself and your students.
• Remember that kids are influenced by their parents: give the kids a break. Schools provide the opportunity to expand horizons.

Our first step in building bridges and knocking down barriers in school is to ask the simple question, "How am I treating you?" Not too dissimilar from what our kids were taught in school, "Stop and think!" Yes, stop and think at the beginning and ending of each day, "How am I treating you?"

8

Religion

*"You can't shake
hands with a closed fist"
- M. Gandhi -*

John Lentz

"True politeness is the spirit of benevolence showing itself in a refined way. It is the expression of good-will and kindness. It promotes both beauty in the man who possesses it, and happiness in those who are about him. It is a religious duty, and should be a part of religious training." - Henry Ward Beecher

She was in tears trying to explain her anguish. A Muslim, she was sharing with an interfaith group called "We Believe" the words of Michael Savage, the host of a nationally syndicated radio program. Savage had gone on an anti-Muslim tirade. *"What kind of religion is this? What kind of world are you living in when you let them in here [USA] with that throwback document [Quran] in their hand, which is a book of hate. Don't tell me I need reeducation. They need deportation."* In an earlier show Savage had said, *"I think [Muslims] need to be forcibly converted to Christianity…it's the only thing that can probably turn them into human beings."*

The rest of this group of Jewish, Christian and Unitarian leaders sat stunned. The very reason we had called ourselves together as an interfaith group was to talk about the kind of compassion, civility, and hospitality that is common to all religious traditions of the world. We had gathered to claim civility in the political process as a spiritual mandate. And yet, we all knew that people who call themselves "religious" can be the most uncivil lot in many cultures. And not only uncivil, but violent, intolerant, and hate-filled, all based on interpretations of their sacred scriptures. From the Crusades to the present religiously fueled terrorism, persons have claimed a blessing from God to do despicable deeds. The incivility of religion is one of the main reasons why people get

WE HAD GATHERED TO CLAIM CIVILITY IN THE POLITICAL PROCESS AS A SPIRITUAL MANDATE. so turned off by faith institutions.

At a recent gathering of clergy where civility was the topic of discussion, one Christian pastor who would call himself a "Bible believer" shared that his church was going to have a converted Jew explain the "real" significance of Passover at a pre-Easter program at church and all were invited. To the rest of the Christian clergy this didn't sound too radical or inhospitable. However the conservative rabbi who was also in attendance was very uncomfortable at this announcement. To him, this declaration implied that his tradition, for which Passover is the central act of identity, was neither being recognized nor respected. It took a great deal of courage for him to speak up and let the rest of us know his feelings. With great gentleness but firmness, he reminded us that not everyone in the room agreed or felt welcomed by the invitation.

Many mainstream denominations within the Christian tradition are being rent asunder by the issue of the ordination of gay, lesbian and trans-gendered persons. Oftentimes, disagreement leads to the worst kinds of uncivil behavior among those who purportedly know better. People are stereotyped, degraded, their very identities as "real believers" questioned as the rhetoric builds. It is not easy to tackle hot-button issues when the matters of faith and perceived "truth" are concerned. However, it should be the goal of faith-based organizations, as well as secular ones, to witness to something deeper than name-calling and partisanship.

Almost all people claim the Golden Rule - do unto others as you would have them do unto you - as one of the foundations of their faith perspective. It is pretty easy to apply the Golden Rule to those who agree with our interpretation of scripture; that is expected. Most people of faith also believe that it is important to be polite to those with whom we disagree. However, civility is more profound than simply being polite. If we believe that someone's lifestyle or belief system is evil, sinful, or dangerous, then surface politeness is mere window dressing, just a cover-up for our true feelings.

I believe that genuine civility calls for something much more profound: a sincere effort to challenge and change these underlying feelings. It is risky but worth it. As mentioned at the outset of this book, the prophet Micah lived almost 3,000 years ago. He called the Jewish people at that time to hear what God really wanted: *"He has told you, O mortal, what is good; and what does the Lord require of you but to do justice, and to love kindness, and to walk humbly with your God?"* (Micah 6:8) Micah's words are prescient in our day still. For one of the underlying pillars of living a truly civil life is to live a humble one too. Humility comes

HOWEVER, IT SHOULD BE THE GOAL OF FAITH-BASED ORGANIZATIONS, AS WELL AS SECULAR ONES, TO WITNESS TO SOMETHING DEEPER THAN NAME-CALLING AND PARTISANSHIP.

from the core word *humus*, which is the rich dark soil that everyone wants in their garden. Good soil bears good fruit. For the religious person, humility is at the core of faith. We understand that

FOR ONE OF THE UNDERLYING PILLARS OF LIVING A TRULY CIVIL LIFE IS TO LIVE A HUMBLE ONE TOO. God is bigger than any single conception that we have in our minds: God is larger than any of our interpretations. Furthermore, it is a core belief that every person is made in God's image and therefore worthy of deepest respect. Humility invites us to gentle care for one another and compassion. It may be that the actions of another mystify us, but in most cases civility calls us to suspend our judgment and press for deeper knowledge.

A devout Christian friend once said to me, "John, they don't have to be wrong for us to be right." So all people of faith are called to claim their perspective with deepest conviction, but that doesn't have to lead to a right/wrong or us versus them worldview. We need a combination of hope and faith that appreciates the variety of perspectives, trusting that in the sharing, some truth larger than any of us can see at the moment will emerge.

People who are part of a civil society must be grounded in the *humus* of humility. How can we curse a neighbor, or ignore someone in need, or tell a crude joke, or flip someone off, or even condemn another to hell if the root of our being is anchored in the rich soil of love and humility? What we find when we are uncivil to each other is that we have created a hell of our own making.

Religious communities have a significant investment in teaching their children the value of human life, the ethics of kindness, humility, justice, and civility. It would seem one of the first tasks of religious education is NOT

HUMILITY COMES FROM THE CORE WORD HUMUS, WHICH IS THE RICH DARK SOIL THAT EVERYONE WANTS IN THEIR GARDEN. GOOD SOIL BEARS GOOD FRUIT. FOR THE RELIGIOUS PERSON, HUMILITY IS AT THE CORE OF FAITH.

in teaching how other faiths are wrong but in grounding our own faith tradition in an appreciation of other faith traditions. It is an historic fact that Judaism planted the seeds from which sprouted both Christianity and Islam. This fact alone would suggest a civil attitude one to another. One doesn't have to work too hard to find many areas of similarity between the Abrahamic faiths and Buddhism and Sikhism among the eastern religions. Surely there are differences, but the common threads that unite us as humans call us towards a profound civility.

At a recent meeting a guest speaker shared a fact that I found most disturbing. The statistic revealed the kind of work that needs to be done if we are to claim civility as a grounding force in our society. It was reported that 70% of respondents to a recent survey claimed that they were "…not interested in learning about other people's faith." (Belief Net Survey 2005)

The good news is that there are many hopeful signs that civility is beginning to reclaim its foundation as a core value of faithful people. Let me share some of the good news with you.

WE UNDERSTAND THAT
GOD IS BIGGER THAN ANY
SINGLE CONCEPTION THAT
WE HAVE IN OUR MINDS:
GOD IS LARGER THAN ANY
OF OUR INTERPRETATIONS.

1. The Values Group

The church that I serve is a mainstream Presbyterian church on the left side of most theological and political issues. However, I celebrate the very faithful, active, and vocal minority who would call themselves "conservatives." One of the blessings of serving my congregation is that we heartily disagree about a whole range of topics but almost always return to our deepest conviction that God is love and there is room at the table for everyone. However, before the election of 2004, I could feel something amiss in the spirit of the community. The tension we felt around the war in Iraq, the rise of the so-called "value voters," the controversy about claiming our faith in the public arena was building to an unhealthy level.

A few weeks before the election, I invited one and all to an evening conversation entitled "Faith and Politics." My goal was to engage people in a positive conversation about the political issues that were most important to them and the biblical verses and theological questions that were reflected in these political issues. Furthermore, I wanted those who attended to share their own stories so that all could come to understand that opinions, no matter how deeply held, are shaped by the text of their lives. Twenty-five people showed. Unfortunately twenty-three of them were for candidate Kerry and two were as yet undecided but left leaning; it was hardly the diversity of opinion that I had hoped for. It isn't hard to be civil to those with whom you agree. Still, that night wasn't a waste. We answered the questions, shared our stories, found variations of opinions, and agreed that discussions like this must take place more often.

But the question of how to get a more diverse group together stayed with me. Was it the case that folks with an alternative opinion believed that they would not have been heard so they didn't even bother to come? Perhaps in our hope of being hospitable, inclusive and civil to all, we were, in fact, giving off clues that we were not really any of these things. Our best intentions did not match, in fact, the way we actually did things.

After the election, the country's choice came down to a few precincts in a few states, and the post-election scramble was marred by incivility. This time, I decided to hand pick a group of twenty members, making sure that political and theological diversity were represented. At the first meeting, I asked the participants to share what they valued about our congregation. Almost everyone agreed that we are welcoming and active in deepening our faith and being involved in the community. Everyone recognized that we value children and have a great music program. We left that first meeting appreciative of the community that we call our faith home. In the weeks that followed, the group of twenty winnowed itself to a dozen. We learned more about each other. We invited a qualified conflict trainer to come and train us how to express our deepest convictions without pointing fingers and diminishing the conviction of others. We practiced our skills on some "hot button" issues like the war, abortion, and gay marriage. We read the Hebrew prophets (Micah and Amos) together and studied the beatitudes of Jesus (Matthew 5:1-48, Luke 6:17-49). In time, what happened was this: the group began to celebrate and anticipate the perspectives and opinions of each member from the most conservative to the most liberal. Our focus became less about who was right or wrong and more about caring for each other. The group wrote a document entitled the "Values Document" in which we articulated core values that would shape our conversations, indeed our lives (Forest Hill Church, Presbyterian 2007 www.fhcpresb.org.)

2. We Believe

During the same time that the Values Group was meeting, the interfaith group called We Believe mentioned at the beginning of this chapter was formed in Northeast Ohio. Downstate in Columbus, a coalition of Christian churches and their pastors claimed the title "The Patriot Pastors." Their stated goal was to convert Ohio to Christianity and to make sure that elected state officials followed their narrow goals shaped by one interpretation of scripture. Needless to say, non-Christians as well as many Christians were frightened by the rhetoric of exclusion, the implication that Ohio was only for some citizens and not for all. The issue was not so much one's faith shaping one's politics but suggesting that one particular religious opinion was going to set the single platform for the entire state. And so the call went out in Columbus and in Cleveland. And religious leaders, clergy and congregant, Jewish, Muslim, Protestant and Catholic, Sikh, Buddhist, Unitarian came together to witness to another way. We did not agree on many specifics and some disagreed on particular issues, but all believed that what we held in common was more important than what divided us. (To see the mission statement for We Believe, please go to www.webelieveohio.org). In the months that passed we gathered monthly and shared a common vision. We discussed issues of concern and held forums on the minimum wage and the death penalty, inviting representatives from each of the faith traditions to share their particular perspectives. We ate at each other's houses and attended each other's parties. We began an initiative called "Make Ohio a Political Sleaze-Free Zone," stressing the importance of civility in politics where stereotyping, scape-goating, distortion, and negative campaign ads were a violation of our faith values and beneath the dignity of the voter and the candidate. In the first three weeks of the initiative over 1,000 people signed a petition declaring Ohio a sleaze-free zone.

3. The Presbytery Meeting

An opportunity to put these concepts of civility to practice presented itself to The Presbytery of the Western Reserve in Northeast Ohio, which has struggled over the issue of the ordination of gay, lesbian and transgendered (GLBT) persons for decades. Lines are drawn depending on how one interprets scripture and how one defines "sin," "family values," and what God wants; these lines are hard to step over. Folks who were once friends find it hard to talk. Meetings can become divisive and frustrating, as both sides offer exasperated sighs. "Do we have to talk about this again?" In many places, individual congregations are separating from the denominations and joining other like-minded congregations. This issue has created an atmosphere where like-minded people sit with like-minded people, and people in the minority find themselves marginalized and called names that hardly do justice to their deepest faith convictions. But two pastors decided to do a new thing. One is a man and one is a woman. One is conservative and one is liberal. One has a congregation in a still-rural but fast-growing community. The other had a congregation in an inner-ring suburb and is now an organizer for a Presbyterian group supporting the ordination of GLBT. They have nothing in common except the faith that they hold dear and the church that they love. They decided to start having lunches together. The lunches were not to debate but to share stories, personal needs, hopes, dreams and fears. Treating each other with a civility that is grounded in their faith, they became friends. One even recommended the other to be the representative of the Presbytery at the bi-annual gathering of the denomination. Each made a commitment to reach out to others with whom they disagreed on this issue, and they challenged every member of the Presbytery to do the same. It has made a difference.

PRACTICING CIVILITY CHANGES LIVES, CHANGES ORGANIZATIONS AND CHANGES COMMUNITIES.

The quality of our meetings has changed. There is more humor, more room for differences and shared vision. Will this model of civility move the issue of ordination along? Who knows? But it cannot hurt. For those who wait for clarity and decision, patience is required. But who knows what deep currents of trust, hope, faith and love are being stirred by the simple act of having lunch and treating one another with respect?

Practicing civility changes lives, changes organizations and changes communities. It takes a great deal of courage to step out of the bounds of conventionality and seek out the 'other,' to see your neighbor, your enemy, your self as someone worthy of being civil to, at least until the wall that divides us is broken down. One would think that the religious community would be a perfect location for this kind of courage, for it is part of our respective traditions. It is my hope that the seed of civility that has been planted will bear a rich harvest.

9

Sport
The era of the parent

Ron Schmidt

Sport, in this country and across the world, is a microcosm of the society in which we live. It provides entertainment as well as life-learned lessons. Daily it demonstrates how people are treated; professionals, elite athletes and especially our kids. What I would like to focus on is our kids and the part parents and coaches play in all of this. "How am I treating you?" needs to be asked by every parent and coach every day as they are involved in transporting kids to practices and games and as they watch and coach on the sidelines. Every parent and every coach should model respect and civility.

Watching sport in this country can be exhilarating. It can also be depressing to witness the behavior of fans and players, and, in recent years, parents. But it is important to know we can have an effect on this. As parents and coaches, we can respond to and reflect on our actions and behavior. So, how are we treating our kids?

In today's climate, we see problems with parent behavior. One can look at the daily news and hear of some incident where a parent's behavior has crossed the line. Youth hockey and baseball have witnessed parents attacking officials, coaches, and other parents. This is unacceptable. Youth sport is really about a kid participating in something larger than himself or herself, building relationships and making friends. The goal of sport is to develop values and have experiences that the young person will be able to use as a building block for life. It shouldn't be more complicated than that. The goal of a community's sports program should be to teach life skills on the field and off. Even though the nature of sports is competitive and there is nothing wrong in

THE GOAL OF SPORT IS TO DEVELOP VALUES AND HAVE EXPERIENCES THAT THE YOUNG PERSON WILL BE ABLE TO USE AS BUILDING BLOCKS FOR LIFE.

winning, we can all agree that there is an honorable way to compete and be both a winner and a loser.

With that in mind, the baseball awards I gave to my 7-8 year old players were entitled the 2008 Civility Friendship Award. This title was inscribed on each trophy along with the player's name and the name of the league. In addition, each player received a baseball card of him or herself. The baseball card identified both the player's playing skill AND his or her personality skill, like helping and respecting others.

Here's how one of the cards read:

CLEVELAND HEIGHTS
BASEBALL LEAGUE / ROYALS
2008 CIVILITY FRIENDSHIP AWARD
THINKS THE BEST / DARIUS
Be generous to the angel in all of us.
Think the best of your fellow humans
and act accordingly. Darius always
thinks the best of his team and family.

The other players' awards had the following values:
• **LISTENS CAREFULLY**
• **SPEAKS KINDLY**
• **INCLUDES OTHERS**

- **SHOWS EMPATHY**
- **SHOWS RESPECT**
- **TELLS THE TRUTH**
- **SEEKS AGREEMENT**
- **ACCEPTS RESPONSIBILITY**
- **SHOWS COURTESY**
- **RESPECTS OTHERS' OPINIONS**
- **HELPS OTHERS ACHIEVE**
- **APPRECIATES OTHERS**

You might ask, "These are 7-8 year-olds, do they really get this?" First, never underestimate kids these days. But in reality, these trophies were only partly for the kids. They were first and foremost for the parents. They sent a message to the parents that this is what sport is all about: this is what the child walks away with after her high school or collegiate career is over. This is the building block for life.

Leo Dorocher once said the famous line, "nice guys finish last." Perhaps that is even true, to a degree, at the professional level. However, my teams won league titles and shaped the lives of young men and women in positive ways, and that after all is the goal. The recent book by Jeffery Marx, *Season of Life*, shows a perennial high school football championship program grounding its success by shaping young men of distinction and civility who care for each other. Yes, I learned to turn the double play and I could throw out a guy stealing second, but in my career in business I don't do that any more. However, learning to respect an opponent and play with a team has had lasting importance to me.

LESSONS FROM A COACH:

I was 6 years old when I started playing baseball in the 1950s. Certainly life and sport have changed in many ways from when I started. However the fundamentals are the same. There are the kid, the coach, and the parent. I played my last year of Little League Baseball in a little coal mining Appalachian town. The league was formed by a man in 1953 who said, "We kept the parents out of it." Harry is in his 80's today, and I wish his wisdom could influence all the parents of today. Harry said parents could come watch the games but had to remember the games are for the kids, not the parents. Harry is an incredible guy, having fought at Normandy, the Battle of the Bulge, and the Battle of the Hurtgen Forest. He also had the insight and leadership to form the first integrated Little League program in the South.

Today we see so many abuses of kids by parents, coaches, officials, and other parents. Sometimes these parents didn't play sports and don't have a framework of what's right and wrong. Sometimes they are living life through their kids. Sometimes they think a sporting event is where they don't have to think about their actions. To be sure, all of us are influenced by the sport experiences we have had. For me, it's a part of who I am as a professional, part of my identity. Sports participation can have a very positive affect on us as well as a negative, so let's see that it is positive.

My message for parents: let your kids be kids, let your kids figure things out for themselves, and sit back and watch your kids have fun. What you may not realize is that they are doing more than just having fun. They

MY MESSAGE FOR PARENTS: LET YOUR KIDS BE KIDS, LET YOUR KIDS FIGURE THINGS OUT FOR THEMSELVES, AND SIT BACK AND WATCH YOUR KIDS HAVE FUN. are developing discipline, a work ethic, and learning teamwork - meaning they are not the most important person.

They are making lifelong friends and measuring how they stack up in physical and leadership abilities. They are learning to respect themselves and others. If you haven't played competitive sport in this country, you may not realize how it builds a person for lifetime. What I learned on a high school football team equipped me for life.

While I could write a book on what I learned as a player and coach, I will share just two stories from my youth. Parents were not involved in either of these two life experiences.

LESSON IN LEADERSHIP:

When I was fourteen, we moved from our Appalachian town to the city. I was a freshman, and I didn't know a soul at my school. On my first day of summer football practice, I was quite a sight: the freshmen were given the hand me downs, and I weighed all of 105 pounds. After practice, I was in the locker room and a guy across the room asked me my name. He kind of laughed when I replied and said, "That's a funny name." To which I replied, "What's yours?" He replied, "Harvey Metzelbaum," to which I replied, "That's funny, too."

Turns out the guy who was befriending me was the senior captain of the football team, and Harvey was not his name. But that story got legs, and Harvey became my nickname all through high school. By the end of the first day of football practice, before school started, I had an identity. Other kids called me Harvey, coaches did, and future friends of mine did also.

So here was the captain of the football team, not hazing but affirming and befriending the smallest and newest kid on the team. That's civility. That's leadership. That's what sport is all about. And as a reminder to parents, not one parent was involved in this. Hard to believe? Does it happen today? Couldn't tell you. I'm not in the locker rooms today. I'm a parent and I shouldn't be in there anyway.

BE THE COACH:

During my last year of Little League baseball in the coal mining town, a couple of things happened that did not have to do with parents or coaches. I was 11 years old and still couldn't hit the baseball. I used to pray. I did everything, but I just couldn't hit the ball. One day, before going to the plate, as I started the ritual prayers, the thought came to me, "Do you really think God cares whether you can hit a baseball or not?" Part of what sport is all about is relying on one's self. Sure, we get strength from God, but at the end of the day we need to do it ourself and have the confidence. From that next plate appearance, I could not "not" hit a baseball. Not only that, I could place it anywhere it was pitched.

I also learned to hit a curveball at 11 years old, all by myself. No coach or batting instructor taught me; I taught myself. If I hadn't taught myself, I probably wouldn't have played. At the time I didn't think much about it, but today when I consider my experiences, I realize they were very empowering. What a feeling of accomplishment. Every kid needs to feel this same sense: that they can figure out things themselves, without parents. Today, if a parent has a kid who can't hit, he's off to clinics and instructors. Never does the kid get the satisfaction that she or he can do it himself or herself.

So at the end of the day, the best coach and the best parent is the one who empowers the kids to teach themselves, to be their own coaches. Whether your kid gets the college scholarship or not, at some point in time you are not going to be there for them. They need to fend for themselves; they need to be their own coach. That's empowering, much healthier in the long run than taking them to all the camps and instructors. Oh and by the way, the best coaches are attracted to those kids who have become their own coach, who take and show responsibility. Those are the kids that they don't have to coddle. They can teach the squeeze play or the decoy to second to the kid that is ready to go to the next level.

Predicting whether interest rates will go up or down is simple compared to the challenge of raising and nurturing our kids. It can be both very rewarding and very discouraging. Sport should teach life lessons to all our kids. Let's take my friend Harry's advice: step back

SO AT THE END OF THE DAY, THE BEST COACH AND THE BEST PARENT IS THE ONE WHO EMPOWERS THE KIDS TO TEACH THEMSELVES, TO BE THEIR OWN COACHES.

and let our kids realize who they are and let them enjoy their lives. That's our job as the parent and coach of our kids.

10

Business

It's all about relationships

Ron Schmidt

If we treat our employees well, and they treat our customers as they would want to be treated, the organization will be successful in the long run.- An often forgotten business tenet.

To **get** the best service – **befriend** the server
To **give** the best service – **befriend** the customer

This chapter is the culmination of my thoughts and observations from working in corporate America, owning a business, having partners and employees, and observing the operations of hundreds of small businesses. The idea of civility in business sprang from an experimental training we did in our firm several years ago. I am sold on it, along with its competitive bottom line results.

And it IS all about the people. Behind each number is a person who made a decision, provided a service, or produced a product. The people part of business is why the business world continues to engage my mind and spirit. I cherish all my clients for the people they are. That's what has always turned me on about business: the people. And for that privilege, I have felt blessed. A healthy, civil relationship between a company's employees and its customers is critical to the success of the organization. Concrete proof of success exists for companies that stress the importance of the relationship between the employee and the customer. Southwest Airlines reported their 69th straight quarterly profit before the global financial meltdown. Wow! It's been reported time and again that they put their money where their mouth is when it comes to guiding their resources to their customers and employees.

In a recent New York Times article, the headlines read "A Hotel's Secret: Treat the Guests Like Guests." In other words, treat the guests as you would want to be treated. But civility extends to more than just the guests, as the article reported. "Training and staff development are increasingly important not just to make guests happy, but to make staff happy. Keeping staff members loyal and happy has become a concern in a business where turnover rates are 50% for non-management and 25% for management - among the highest of any industry."

In a Q&A, Alan Fuerstman of Montage Hotels and Resorts, was asked, "Can you teach grace and humility?" **A. "Not only do we teach, but we reinforce and reward it. The teaching starts with modeling."**
Q. How do you reinforce that behavior?
A. **"...people commit more acts of kindness when they are appreciated."**
Q. So how do you measure loyalty?
A. "There has been zero turnover in our senior executive team of 14 in 5 years, 10% turnover in management, and 25% in non-management." A 50% advantage in the industry!

Why don't more companies follow this approach? To answer this, let's return to the discussion in Chapter 5 concerning the *foundation of relationships*. The foundation centers on the importance of humanity and the respect for the relationship between the consumer, the employee, and the organization.

What does this foundation look like? In Don Keough's book, *The Ten Commandments for Business Failure*, he

THE FOUNDATION CENTERS ON THE IMPORTANCE OF HUMANITY AND THE RESPECT FOR THE RELATIONSHIP BETWEEN THE CONSUMER, THE EMPLOYEE, AND THE ORGANIZATION.

spells it out very well. "...all business boils down to matters of trust: consumers trust that the product will do what it promises to do, investors trust that management is competent, employees trust management to live up to its obligations." But Mr. Keough laments that the focus in our business marketplace "has moved from managing the company to managing the stock."

In other words, Mr. Keough is concerned that goals and strategies and tactics that organizations implement to improve their bottom line in the short run have replaced the focus on the person, the consumer or the employee, who enhances an organization for the long run. Howard Behar, the former President of Starbucks International, writes in his book *It's Not About The Coffee*, "we're in the people business serving coffee, not the coffee business serving people." In other words, "It's about the people!"

A case can be made that in the financial turmoil that has affected world economies, we have placed profits ahead of people. And those from the "old school" would say we have placed profits ahead of common sense. Instead of starting with the people, the consumer and employee, and working forward, we seem to be focusing on the profit and working backward.

Let's go back to Chapter 5 and reflect on what Virginia Satir might have added today: "...when people gain a new

IN OTHER WORDS, MR. KEOUGH IS CONCERNED THAT GOALS AND STRATEGIES AND TACTICS THAT ORGANIZATIONS IMPLEMENT TO IMPROVE THEIR BOTTOM LINE IN THE SHORT RUN HAVE REPLACED THE FOCUS ON THE PERSON, THE CONSUMER OR THE EMPLOYEE, WHO ENHANCES AN ORGANIZATION FOR THE LONG RUN.

appreciation of their humanity through their relationship with others, it will be demonstrated by how they treat one another." I was recently talking with a woman who "broke into" the business world in the 1940s. She worked in the marketing department of one of the international rubber and tire companies of Akron, Ohio. In her career, with only a high school degree, she traveled the world for that company. I asked her how hard it was for a woman to start out back then. She said it was "surprisingly easy. Back then people took the time to help you out."

So as we lament Don Keough's concerns of managing the stock over the company, what is his message to us? Is he challenging us to take a look at the balance between the bottom line and the relationships within our companies? Do we yield to a craving for profits in the short run at the risk of jeopardizing relationships in the long run? Has the business environment turned our values inside out? Have we forgotten civility?

In order to demonstrate the environment businesses operate in today, let's take an example of a common

AND THOSE FROM THE "OLD SCHOOL" WOULD SAY WE HAVE PLACED PROFITS AHEAD OF COMMON SENSE. INSTEAD OF STARTING WITH THE PEOPLE, THE CONSUMER AND EMPLOYEE, AND WORKING FORWARD, WE SEEM TO BE FOCUSING ON THE PROFIT AND WORKING BACKWARD.

business approach in the service sector: cross-selling. This exists in many industries. In the banking world for instance, cross-selling is the bank's initiative to provide as many of the bank's services to each of its customers. Cross-selling is usually communicated to the customer by a service representative. On paper, it is very straight-forward. Every executive will tell you it is critical for the success of the organization.

But friction sometimes arises between management and the service representative and / or between the representative and the customer. What usually causes the friction is miscommunication and misunderstanding due to a disagreement between the representative and management. Generally the service representative feels conflicted between goals of the organization and needs of the customer. She/he feels trapped somewhere in the middle. Most representatives are conscientious and would err on the side of the customer. Tension arises between what the organization wants the customer to buy and what the customer really needs. And this puts the representative in a "lose-lose" situation.

In order to get at the heart of the disagreement, let's

TENSION ARISES BETWEEN WHAT THE ORGANIZATION WANTS THE CUSTOMER TO BUY AND WHAT THE CUSTOMER REALLY NEEDS. AND THIS PUTS THE REPRESENTATIVE IN A "LOSE-LOSE" SITUATION. step back and ask a few questions. What are we after? Do we want to serve the customer better in the long run or generate profits in the short run? Every executive will tell you that he is always out to serve the long-run interests of the customer, because without customers, he doesn't have a business.

And if the truth be known, those front line people doing the cross-selling are not convinced that cross-selling is good for the customer. If it doesn't feel right to them, and they are the messengers, the message won't be received well by the consumer. That's just human nature. Think about it. If the coach keeps telling the player to throw the curve ball and the kid doesn't have faith that's the right pitch, the results won't be favorable. You'll see the ball go out of the ball park and all your fans-customers go home shaking their heads in disbelief.

So what's the solution? If we cherish the relationship between an organization and the consumer and if our objective is to strengthen it, then we should look to break down barriers in order to make the relationship stronger. I have sold services to clients for over 30 years, and when I'm out there selling something for my own strategic advantage and not theirs, I can see their eyes roll. Our goal with employees and customers is to build bridges, not erect barricades. Building bridges is not only "old

IF WE CHERISH THE RELATIONSHIP BETWEEN AN ORGANIZATION AND THE CONSUMER AND IF OUR OBJECTIVE IS TO STRENGTHEN IT, THEN WE SHOULD LOOK TO BREAK DOWN BARRIERS IN ORDER TO MAKE THE RELATIONSHIP STRONGER.

school"; it is long term and it will build customer loyalty.

As other relationships, it's not what you say as much as how you say it that can be critical in building bridges with employees and customers. How do we approach our customers and employees? Let's start with our employees, for they are the ones engaging with the customer. Do we shout orders at them or do we talk with them as a coach? The job of the coach is to develop the talent she has recruited or inherited and to strengthen the relationships within the company. This is different from shouting orders. Not every executive has that teaching and motivating personality of a coach. It's imperative that someone on the management team have those qualities and that the executive understand that everyone needs a coach. Shouting orders does not strengthen relationships with employees; it only builds barriers. So the job of the CEO is to build bridges with her employees so they in turn build bridges with customers. And remember, the best coaches are themselves the most coachable. If the "coach" is not receptive to differences and new ideas, if the "coach" is not a good listener, if the "coach" communicates by intimidation, it's time to do a little substitution.

In Jeffrey Krames' book, *Inside Drucker's Brain*, he

THE JOB OF THE COACH IS TO DEVELOP THE TALENT SHE HAS RECRUITED OR INHERITED AND TO STRENGTHEN THE RELATIONSHIPS WITHIN THE COMPANY. THIS IS DIFFERENT FROM SHOUTING ORDERS.

quotes Peter Drucker's insight on Jack Welch, the famed former head of General Electric. He stated that while Welch had many good instincts, his most valuable quality was that he was a great listener. In addition, he asked the right question at the right time of the right person. For the executives of the world, the job is to be the best listener and ask the right question, to affirm and respect employees.

In summary, effective communication starts at the top with the coach (top down) who enables the employees to generate the connection with the customer (bottom up). We are in the "people business" where we provide a service or product. As we draft our strategies and tactics, we need to get a grasp on the human nature of employees and customers. We work with employees; we don't shout at them and they don't "serve" us. Once that link is firmly established, the employee-customer relationship will fall naturally in place.

Another place where the relationship with both employees and customers is often challenged is the medical community. The doctor is the authority figure who may not only "dictate" the service but also impose his/her personality vis-a-vis his behavior on the employee and the patient. If he/she is not respectful of others,

IF THE "COACH" IS NOT RECEPTIVE TO DIFFERENCES AND NEW IDEAS, IF THE "COACH" IS NOT A GOOD LISTENER, IF THE "COACH" COMMUNICATES BY INTIMIDATION, IT'S TIME TO DO A LITTLE SUBSTITUTION.

there may be friction which can be injurious to the patient's health. A New York Times article noted surveys of hospital staff members "who blame badly behaved doctors for low morale, stress, and high turnover...Recent studies suggest that such behavior contributes to medical mistakes, preventable mistakes, preventable complications and even death." The survey noted that health care workers from102 nonprofit hospitals between 2004 and 2007 "found that 67% of respondents said they thought there was a link between disruptive behavior and medical mistakes, and 18% said they knew of a mistake that occurred because of an obnoxious doctor." Fear sets into a hostile work environment. A doctor is quoted: "When the wrong surgery is done on patients, often there is somebody in the operating room who knew the event was going to occur and who didn't feel empowered to speak up..."

FOR THE EXECUTIVES OF THE WORLD, THE JOB IS TO BE THE BEST LISTENER AND ASK THE RIGHT QUESTION, TO AFFIRM AND RESPECT EMPLOYEES.

The guiding light of where and how we go in the future should be based on how we treat one another. *Sometimes in business, more often than we want to admit, we become so focused on short-term results that we lose track of what got us there: relationships, i.e. our relationships with our employees, customers, and suppliers.* That's the connector element, that's the people part, that's where our resources should be engaged, in "managing the company" and not "managing the stock," as Don Keough would say.

If you are the executive making decisions that affect your bottom line, what are some due diligence questions you should ask yourself, or expect your management team to ask of one another? Let's not make it too complicated. What are the short term and long term effects on:

1. the consumer
2. the employees
3. the investors
4. the sustainability of the company

Randy Pausch, the professor of computer science, human-computer interaction, and design at Carnegie Mellon, who recently passed away from pancreatic cancer, turned his "last lecture" at the university into a best selling book entitled *The Last Lecture*. He talked to the Associated Press about what his childhood dreams had taught him about life and said, "It's not about how to achieve your dreams, it's about how you lead your life." So as leaders, the question is how you should lead your organizations, first and foremost, that will help them achieve those dreams and goals? And the answer is somewhere in the relationships. Businesses can produce effective change. It starts with the "buy-in" of the executives, and the message to the organization, of the "value of the customer and employee." For the message to become an integral part of the culture, the employees need to feel in control and have ownership. They need to understand the message and make it a part of their life and the life of the organization.

AFTERWORD

John Lentz

I remember when I preached my first sermon at the New York Avenue Presbyterian Church in Washington D.C., thirty years ago. I had a first draft of the sermon ready. Reviewing it with my mother, I was taken aback by one simple question.

She asked, "So what?" I answered, "What do you mean, 'so what?' You don't like it?" And she replied: "Yes, I like it. It isn't bad for a first draft. But...what do you want the listener to do? You don't just want to tell a good story or two. You want your words to have some impact, to effect some change."

Since that conversation I have always tried to have a "so what" ending on my sermons and on all my writing.

"So what?" This is the question that Ron and I are asking ourselves now that we have told you about the Civility Project in Cleveland Heights, Ohio, and shared our opinions about how to treat one another in business, school, politics, sport and religion.

Not only our hope but our presumption is that you look inward and ask yourselves, "How can I be more civil to my spouse, my child, my colleagues, my clients, my students, or the guy who is driving in the car behind me wanting to

104

pass?" We want you to look in the mirror and do some self analysis.

We also want you to have your eyes and ears open. As you go about your day, what do you notice? Are people being civil to each other or is everybody just too rushed to care? How are people treating you and how are you treating them?

Are you experiencing what we shared in the book? Are you hearing others share their yearning for community and courtesy? We want you to consider how your relationships, neighborhoods, and cities might change for the better if you had a block party, reached out to a stranger, or took a simple step toward humility and civility.

So this is more than a story, it is an invitation to look inward and act outward, to be the change you seek. It starts with YOU!

There continue to be so many challenges in our daily lives. Sometimes it is hard to be intentional about treating others the way we want to be treated. It seems we are always taking two steps backwards to go one step forward. And yet, every once in a while, we come across someone doing an act of kindness, we see a commercial on television that emphasizes gentleness and civility, or we hear about an initiative that makes us say to ourselves: "Yes! That is what I am talking about!

SO THIS IS MORE THAN A STORY, IT IS AN INVITATION TO LOOK INWARD AND ACT OUTWARD, TO BE THE CHANGE YOU SEEK. IT STARTS WITH YOU!

If only there were more of that!"

As we have worked on this book and became more sensitized to civility and how people treat one another, Ron and I have seen and heard about many initiatives in this country and across the world where people are rising up and choosing to act in ways that move towards civility, understanding, and hope rather than recrimination, violence and despair. The community project in Duluth, Minnesota, inspired us from our beginnings.

More recently Ron and I traveled to Israel and Palestine. Our first night was spent in the village of Neve Shalom/Wahat al-Salam (Oasis of Peace) in Israel. For the last 35 years this community has been a living example of how we should treat one another. Located on the plains between Tel Aviv and Jerusalem, Wahat al-Salam/Neve Shalom is an intentional community in Israel where Jewish and Palestinian Arab Israeli citizens live and raise their children. This community is committed to demonstrating that Arabs and Jews, Israelis and Palestinians, can live and work together, engage in dialogue and educational outreach aimed at breaking down the barriers that separate them. The "Oasis of Peace" has been nominated five times for the Nobel Peace Prize for its efforts to create a genuine and durable peace by teaching trust, mutual respect, and understanding.

We walked in the school yard and listened to classes taught in both Hebrew and Arabic, saw the children play, and heard about hard work that goes into living together in peace. Yet the same spirit that inspires Neve Shalom/Wahat al-Salam inspires our work as well. There has to be a vision, some sense of a goal that is out there. There has to be intentionality; the vision has to move from drawing board to risk and experiment. There has to be ownership; this can't wait for someone else to do.

Ron and I believe that reflecting on how you treat your neighbor, your spouse or partner, your customer or parishioner may not change the world overnight...but it might. Your smile to a stranger, your "thank-you" to a visitor, your taking a deep breath and NOT expressing the first thing that comes to mind in a stressful situation may not seem like much. *However, just as the melting ice on the hillside joins with other small streams to form a rushing river towards the sea, so too will your act join millions of others, and we will all find our destination in the beloved community called humanity.*

APPENDIX

**The Heights Civility Project
Civility Project's Mission Statement,
Cleveland Heights University Heights, Ohio**
"We believe civility is a fundamental value [1]
of our community.

Civility means to
- listen;
- apologize;
- be aware;
- be inclusive;
- speak kindly;
- show respect;
- tell the truth;
- seek agreement;
- take responsibility;
- accept constructive criticism.

*We believe in taking proactive steps toward civility every day.
We also believe we have the right and responsibility to expect
others to do the same.*

[1] Based on the work of P.M. Forni, author of *"Choosing Civility:
The Twenty-Five Rules of Considerate Conduct."*

Is this an individual or organizational commitment?

_____ Individual _____Organizational

If organizational, what is the name of the organization?
_____

What is your position with the organization?
_____

Name _____

Please Print Name _____

Signature _____

ACKNOWLEDGEMENTS & THANKS

This book took us down many paths and along the way many folks contributed to its success. Dan Porter started the process with us and encouraged us along the way. Many starts and stops later we sat with our editor Kris Ohlson who gave us new direction and motivation. Elspeth Peterjohn and Barbara Israel did for us what retired high school English teachers do; they worked with us on grammar and expression. And in addition we had many "readers" who pointed out "cracks in the pavement." Lissa Waite, Jim Sollisch, Chip Coakley and Mark Siwik gave us crucial insight. Dr. P. M. Forni enlightened us. Our community newspaper, The Sun Press, provided significant coverage to the Civility Project. Reporter Ed Wittenberg and editor Mary Jane Skala were critical to our community support.

We want to recognize the City of Duluth, Minnesota, and the engaging women that made presentations to our city during an early winter snowstorm: Kathy Bartsias, Mary Bridget Lawson and Brenda Sproat.

The success of a community's project is based on leadership. We deeply thank the leaders in our communities and the core committee members of the

Civility Project: Steve Bullock, Renee Cavor, Deb Delisle, Nancy Dietrich, Diane Millett, Ron Register, Rufus Sims, Al Slawson and Meghan Zehnder. Steve Litt of the Cleveland Heights - University Heights Public Library was a strong supporter as well as the Cleveland Heights - University Heights Board of Education. And lastly, we thank Mayors Kelley and Rothschild.

USES FOR THE BOOK

• Individual and group reflection on our behaviors in everyday life

• Discovery and reinforcement of foundational values of an organization or community

• Group discussions

• Recommended reading for everyone in a school, organization, business, congregation or team

• Organizational retreat theme

• Customer service discussions

• Human resources counseling and seminars

• Enhancing an organization's bottom line

QUICK ORDER FORM

- **Fax orders**: 440-248-2902. Send this form please.

- **Telephone orders**: Please call 216-255-1892

- **Website orders**: www.HowAmITreatingYou.com

- **Quantity of order**: _____
(price discounted on orders over 50)

Name: _____

Address: _____

City: _____ State:_____ Zip: _____

Telephone: _____

E-mail address: _____

Sales tax: 7.75% added for books shipped to Ohio address.
Shipping charges: Standard rates apply.

ABOUT THE AUTHORS

How am I Treating You? Living with Civility and Dignity,
is co-authored by two members of The Heights Civility
Project, Ron Schmidt and John Lentz, Jr. Both are
published authors in their resident field of expertise.
Individually their credentials are presented as follows:

Dr. John Lentz, Jr.: graduate of Kenyon College, Yale
University, and Edinburgh University in Scotland;
ordained minister, pastor, published author, community
activist - and champion of any effort that helps develop
the human spirit. He is considered by many as a thought
leader in his field. John's work *Luke's Portrait of Paul* was
published by Cambridge University Press in 1993. John
frequently enters dialogues in the community where he
lends his ability to blend diverse groups into a common
dialogue that underscores the power, potential, and
spiritual nature of our shared humanity. John is the senior
pastor of Forest Hill Church, Presbyterian.

Ron Schmidt: graduate of the University of Kentucky,
University of Louisville, and the Weatherhead School
of Business, Case Western Reserve University. Resident

of Cleveland Heights for thirty years, consultant and business owner, coach, Rotarian, Junior Achievement adviser, and active member on boards and in the community, Ron is a frequent keynote speaker for industry events and is published in industry periodicals. Ron is President of CBS Certified Public Accountants, LLC and Credit Union Business Solutions, LLC.